CLOSER TO NOWHERE

Copyright © Thorpe Moeckel 2025
All rights reserved.

No part of this publication may be reproduced in whole or in part, or stored in a retrieval system, or transmitted in any form or by any means, electronic, mechanical, photocopying, recording, by Artificial Intelligence "training" or data mining, without written permission of the author.

First Edition
ISBN: 978-1-963110-17-3

https://www.thorpemoeckel.com/

Published by
Pine Row Press
www.pinerow.com

For permissions or inquiries, please contact:
Pine Row Press
Ft Mitchell, KY
contact@pinerow.com

CLOSER

TO

NOWHERE

*Lost and Found in the Lower Canyons
of the Rio Grande*

Thorpe Moeckel

Pine Row Press
Ft Mitchell, KY

Contents

1	Current States
5	Water Talks
13	Reef of Feels
23	Overheard
33	Boquillas the Slow Way
47	And Underheard
55	Desert Rain
67	Things to Do When You're Camped for Five Days at San Rosendo Canyon in October and Waiting for the River to Drop Out of Flood
71	Sounds
79	Low Water, Loose Stone
85	And Echoes
93	Like Swimming Underwater Except it Gives You Breath
103	Twice
105	Acknowledgments

for Ola and William

&

for Lee Williams

...si uno dice Dame fuego cuando ellos dicen Dame una luz, ¿qué no se aprende sobre el fuego, la luz y sobre el acto de dar? No es que sea otra manera de hablar de las cosas: son cosas nuevas. Es el mundo sucediendo nuevamente, advierte Makina: prometiendo otras cosas, significando otras cosas, produciendo objetos distintos.

—Yuri Herrera

...if you say Give me fire when they say Give me a light, what is not to be learned about fire, light and the act of giving? It's not another way of saying things: these are new things. The world happening anew, Makina realizes: promising other things, signifying other things, producing different objects."

—Yuri Herrera (trans. Lisa Dillman)

Current States

O this on the map, off the map feeling
—Juliana Spahr

SILTY AND SLOW WATER, SHORT, EASY STROKES. A GENTLE breeze. The river sluggish and low. Often you pause and hold a quiet steering stroke. No hurry, none at all.

The mountains ahead, they aren't small. You look at the map and then look back up at the bow, the river ahead, and then beyond. You'll enter the canyon soon. The light will be different there, everything will be different there, as it already is here.

One side of the river, the north side, is beige on the map, with words and lines, creeks, trails, place names, roads. The south side of the river, though, is blank, as in no words, no lines, no landmarks, nothing—blank.

Strange plants, strange, sinuous landforms. And stone. The ground infinite bits of stone, every piece beautiful in its way. Mosaic upon mosaic. Layers.

Feels, is what, a swirl of thoughts and feels. Upwellings. Canyon feels, border feels, which are also captivity feels, of an extended between. Many betweens. Between times. Between cliffs, currents, countries, lives.

As in: Between fire and no fire, when there is no wood left. Or when there is no heat to start the fire, though lots of wood. Or there is not enough oxygen to allow the heat and fuel to breathe.

Estrangement, this, intimate estrangement, knowing and unknowing felt in the body, so many feels, the being a touching, a being touched, names and labels isolated so that one might slow them, be touched—anew, estranged—by them.

Another camp, where you'll stay for another night, too. You have many days, more river to travel, camps to come. Much driftwood, easy to gather. You burn wood and watch the fire and the moon, and sometimes you read.

Between conception and birth, birth and death.

To unknow the shape of what stands between. To unknow the between. Even to unknow the unknowing. Blank space. Blank. No roads, no names, no lies, feels, lines, home.

Between suffering and joy, fear and love, light and shadow, blood and flesh, mind and body, coupled and uncoupled, poetry and prose, them and us. Between in love and out of love. Understanding and ignorance. Clarity and dismay. Reader and writer. Fable and fact. Now here and nowhere. Alone and not alone. So many betweens.

For now, there's only this place, the materiality of it and of the language of the place, utterances and gestures. There is the map, as useful for what it leaves out as for what it tries to show. Also, the canoe, its slow leak.

As in: When two bodies stand in proximity between the moon and the ground, the borders between those bodies as expressed by the shadow grow indistinct, fused, as if one.

As in: Between a love that is borderless, that acknowledges fear (calls it fear), that might save us, and a love that draws lines.

As in: That eddy at the inside of the bend, what's floating there, the swirls.

And if the history of names is a history of many borders, etymological, political, of breath and experience going back very far, to when we moved from grunts and body language to shaping our breath around our experience, and finding commonalties in that breath-shaping, establishing patterns, breathmaps, borders—language itself—well, what then? And what now?

To feel the between. To unfeel the border and breathe the between. Empty space. Blank. No roads, no names, no lines.

As in: Between self and no self, where accepting that thoughts are independent of the thinker (it is the thought that thinks, it is wisdom not the wise that realizes) might lead to a more borderless presence, a presence where thoughts cross borders of selves, because there are no borders between the selves, as there are no selves.

Only patience, books, food, a decent paddle, health. And the blue canoe, which lets the river in a little bit at a time. It's enough, plenty.

As in: Silt. Feels of silt along the many spectrums of being in place.

THIS PLACE WHERE OUR breath is paused, the lungs empty or the lungs full, is the sacred, the lost, the between place. But is it between? Or is the taking in and letting out of breath the between?

How with enough time, luck, and love, you might be able from afar to create from memory the feel of the river's body.

On the spectrums of being in place, breathing it in or you are breathing it out or you are holding it in or out.

And because every river's a swarm of borders (between placid and turbulent, reflection and depth, rising and falling, and so on), the river is riding you the way the border is crossing you, and you are riding, riding on and in and across these currents and many more each day and night as you do your thing.

And yet: So many lines always being drawn. Lines of trespass. Lines of accusation. Persecution lines. Shaming lines. Distortion lines. Fear and falsehood lines. Lines of credit, debt, borrowing, lending. Loss lines. So much loss. Righteousness lines. Delusion lines. You've-gone-way-overboard lines.

AND SOME STAND AT a border and ask: What kind of mischief can I get away with over there?

And some ask: What might I bring back to show others?

Or: What lessons for living might I bring back from over there?

How might I be of service over there?

Or: What's the nature of the border itself?

From the same root as board, but board as referring to an old ship's perimeter, the place that marks the line between sea and deck, danger and safety.

Also has roots in reference to the outer edge of a shield, beyond which the enemy's weapon can harm you.

AND THEN THERE ARE borders of feeling, infinite feelings and infinite borders, spectruming between solitude and loneliness, grief and sadness, lust and longing, anger and passion, confusion and compassion — more porous, these borders?

Because a river reaches far beyond its channel, because to know a river means doing the same.

And what of borders of meaning, as in how the word border, for example, can mean very different things from one person to the next (as well as to one person at differing parts of their life).

The cacti, the birds, the ghosts, the shadows, the critters, the stones, their colors, manners. The map is alive now, always has been, but you're living in it, have pitched a tent in it, there and now here. You're exploring deep into its sidecanyons. It's quiet here. There are voices. Many sharp things. Every smell has an edge.

Water Talks

> The garfish and mudfish that you might pull from these waters look primitive, but a catfish only looks embryonic, slack bodied and unossified.
>
> —Franklin Burroughs

MORE RAIN, THE WATER RISING, AND A RED LEAF, SWIRLING with the current on its way to who knows where, said Creek, you are more full than I've ever seen you.

You are more red than I've ever seen you, said creek.

You've seen me? asked red leaf.

Creek said, I see you every year.

How do you know it's me? asked leaf.

Your shape, creek said, is distinctive.

My shape is not my red, said red leaf.

Your red, said creek, is very much your shape.

That's like saying your current is your temperature, began red leaf, or that your rocks are your water's taste.

Why not say it then? asked creek.

Because it isn't true, said red leaf.

What is true lies beyond distinctions, said creek.

Perhaps within, rather than beyond them, is where the truth lies, red leaf said.

Or the truth is born from them, said creek.

Are you saying truth is both born in and beyond distinctions? asked red leaf.

I'm saying truth is born in what lies beyond form, said creek, before distinctions but at the heart of them too.

That is thick stuff, creek, said red leaf.

It is day of thick flow, said creek.

I feel it, said red leaf. I am powerless with feeling it.

You are indeed the opposite, red leaf, said creek. You are all power now.

How so, if I am soon to be one more leaf now bunched among other leaves against a stone? asked red leaf.

You are becoming, said creek.

I am being undone, began red leaf, along with many other leaves.

You are becoming, said creek.

Flood me, said red leaf. Just flood me till I'm all undone.

Such a request, creek said, is power.

Catfish munched some yum as it moseyed along the little eddy's silty bottom. Soon, it came upon a new thing. In years of days of finding food, catfish had never sensed such a thing in the river. River, catfish asked, what is this thing?

It's not a rock, said river.

I know that, said catfish, and I know it's not a soggy bit of wood, either.

It sort of is, said river.

Is what? asked catfish.

A soggy bit of wood, said river. A soggy bit of a lot of bits of wood, more like.

What's it called, this thing? asked catfish.

A book, said river.

Something lost, you mean, wondered catfish, something human?

Like the shoes you bump sometimes, said river, and other lost things, yes, human.

It feels flooded, said catfish.

Good, said river, but it can also run very low.

What do you mean? asked catfish. What, anyway, is a book?

A way for humans to share stories.

Without talking?

Yes. The talk is preserved through ink in the paper, and the paper is made of ground up wood. The humans can read the inktalk like you read the bottom of the river, for nourishment, lessons, wonders, feels.

Feels? asked catfish.

Feels, yes, river said. Feels like, like laughter, tears, love, curses. Even prayers.

May I read it? asked catfish.

I don't know, said river. Give it a try.

THE SPRING AND THE river were oldest of friends. They often discussed matters. The spring's water was clear and the river's water was the color of silt. The springwater emerged, warmer than the river water, and then trickled through silt and roots into the milky, gray river; a little mist rose there. It was morning. The river spoke. It is another day, said the river.

The spring said, Do the days ever end? The river, with a crease and a pulsing wave abloom on its spine, looked askance at the spring. I mean, the spring said, you say it is another day but is it really another day? Can't it be one long day, with alternating darkness and light. Why must each change of dark to light be called another day? It gets tiresome, I think.

You muddle my water with such thinking, said the river.

Ha, the spring said. I am the clearer of the waters, by far.

Clear water, said the river, does not make for clear thinking.

I'm sorry to have mentioned it. Why compare, anyway? Water is water. We all bear our loads. My water bears heat and minerals, yours silt.

The question of the days is a curious one, the river said.

I was just being curious, said the spring.

We must stay curious, said the river. Thank you for reminding me.

Darkness and light, the spring said, and then darkness and light.

For some, it is always darkness, said the river. For others, it is light and light and more light.

Isn't it a question of love, asked the spring.

Isn't it always, the river noted.

It is, but when is it a question of a love that will not die? the spring said. Where is the love that will not die?

It is here, I hear it, it is what we do, no? the river said. We never cease. We are at the bottom of everything. Everything moves down through us.

But I move up, the spring said.

You move up from great depths, warm depths, the river said, to bring a moment, nothing more, of clarity and warmth to those moving down, closer to the love that will not die.

It was August. The stream ran low but was busy with creatures seeking to cool off. One day, a little human stood on the bank, and sneezed, and a virus entered the stream.

The stream said, Are you singing?

Virus said, I am host seeking.

Sounds like a dirge, stream said, but what sort of host do you seek?

A warm one, said the virus.

I have been warming for weeks. Am I not a host, said stream.

You are a vehicle, said virus.

I am the lowest point, said stream.

And you move to lower places, where my hosts often like to dwell in large numbers, said virus.

We have passed several creatures warmer than me, just now a beaver, earlier a bathing human, both of them very warm, their orifices exposed, and yet you are still with me.

There is chance involved, said virus.

In the design of your host seeking, said stream, is chance?

Yes, in my design, and in all designs.

And what becomes of a warm body upon its hosting you?

It feeds me. It heats up as it feeds me. It must not burn too hot, however. My main concern is that it remain alive, hot and alive, and it must not understand me deeply enough to annihilate me.

I do not like the sound of your work, said stream.

It is a strange life, and I did not choose it, said virus.

Might you find another vehicle soon? asked stream.

Soon, I will find a host and it will be my vehicle.

A vehicle that also feeds you—how convenient!

But isn't the rain what feeds you while also being what keeps you going?

I suppose, stream said.

Even the light feeds us as it transports us, said virus.

Seems we're all so well hosted and fed, said stream.

It is good to be aware, said virus.

But not too aware, said stream.

Exactly, said virus.

THE GROUND HAD BEEN slowly warming for a few weeks. The earliest flowers were in bloom. Now it was evening. A slow rain had been falling for hours, and one of the spring peeper frogs was emerging after a winter under the mud.

The rain said, How's the world look?

Everything looks the same but more tilted, said peeper.

And what of the fragrance? said rain.

There is the blossom smell and there is the scent of fear.

And what does fear smell like?

Oil.

Is it a fearful smell?

It is not. There's beauty in it.

The rain, does it taste the same, said rain.

It tastes curious.

How is the singing for mates this year?

It feels less hospitable but more spirited.

What about the paleness of the sky?

There is fever in it.

The quality of your hunger.

Slightly fermented, said peeper, and yet of a higher altitude.

The presence of your predators?

Dusky.

Any other questions I need to ask you?

Will this interview be edited?

As you like.

And will it reach an audience?

Of course, said rain. Can't you hear them extending their distance?

THERE WAS A PLACE where water often flowed but there was no water flowing there now. There was mud. There were stones. There were insects and sticks. A bird landed now on a stone at this place and sought to munch some insects.

Hey, bird, said a moth, why don't you go where the water is?

There is more food here, said the bird to the moth.

I think there is more by the river, said moth, kindness in its voice. It's not far. I was just there. It was swarming.

The river is too noisy, said the bird. I like it better here behind the island.

What island? asked the moth.

Said bird, Those trees there, they are an island.

Not now, not with this channel all dried out, said moth.

Said bird, I call it an island. Most of the year this channel is running water.

I call it, said moth, I call it the river. All of it's the river.

How can you call it that? That's sort of nuts, said the bird.

For most of time this was all a river. For way longer back than those who made us or made those who made us or made them. For back before maybe there were even moths or birds, it was all a river.

I've heard that, said bird. But way way back, before the way back, wasn't there an ocean here, too?

Probably, said moth. But an ocean is just a mess of rivers.

THE SNOW WAS STILL falling on the river. The snow had been falling hard all night and through the day. The banks had grown taller from how much snow had fallen, and there were islands of ice floating downstream like soggy pieces of a jigsaw puzzle. As it drifted down, one particular snowflake asked the river, Where will you take me when I land in you?

The river was taking an otter into its right flank but replied after a moment, It's more that you'll take me. I don't know where that'll be.

The snowflake said, I don't understand. You seem to be taking all the flakes and the slushy ice-islands downriver. You just took that otter, too.

It is not so, said the river. What is so, is that there is a movement downstream and many call it the river, but I am a voice, nothing greater or lesser than that, not a river, not a body of water, simply a voice that happens to be speaking right now with a snowflake about to enter the movement downstream and an otter already having moved into it.

Closer to the river than before but still a good ways above it now, the snowflake said, So I'll be joining a movement?

Looks to me like you've already joined, the river said. You're moving aren't you?

I'm falling, said the snowflake, and when I land I'll be moving. There's a difference.

I suppose, said the river, because the movement downstream is rising. You're going to help it rise a little bit more.

I don't know what it's like to be part of a rise

It's all movement, rising not so different from falling, said the river.

The snowflake said, I think there are differences, I think there are some massive differences.

You're being dramatic, the river said.

The snowflake said, It's all movement then, differences not so different from non-differences.

Oneness, muttered the river, is that what we're getting at, oneness?

Otherness? asked the snowflake. What?

Sure, river said, and otterness, too.

Reef of Feels

Only what's human can truly be alien.
The rest is mixed forest, undermining moles, and wind.
—Wislawa Szymborska (trans. Joanna Trzeciak)

this inhospitable land to let it ignore us in
at indian head outside terlingua to begin
let it unlearn us any of terra lingua any

lingua mesquite creosote lingua to let it reveal
stills these harsh basaltic arms clastic influx shallow shales
or not to let it know us something true about surface

silences so post-tidal more quiet than lonesome some
pigmentissima in c chihuahua's now desert's d
to let not butte chalk us in cretaceous sedimentary

no rain some stain one sharp thing after another
until it all looks smooth to let this land have nothing for
us & give the beams & shafts blown out lava tubes breaks in

clouds petroglyphic moon most half again mesa in near
ground the high long peaks beyond breeze from the east nothing sub
compact if the ocean's retreated the sea's still here hear

☙

ocotillo to let the greenery how sparse a
bit of riparian zone growth ducks heron vermillion
flycatcher radio from a truck by a hot springs steam

the rio grande/bravo del norte the feel each riffle
under our loaded canoe to let this be our passport
another forward stroke another silent J swirls me-

anderings mouth boquillas canyon two paloverde
rivercane a sand gravel bluff to let upstream be north
here sky these deadhorse mountains sierra del caballo

muerto hoofprints where hauled the boat up stones higher flows
made smooth so many borders spilling sediment shadow
eons compressed to let the softest things be furthest down

look out from high over the river at how the dust silt
gets laid down after water flush drops inside of the bends
cobblepocked beaches layers vagrant levels wavering

☙

distillate of once lagoon seabed uplift lord knows
this clarity sound travels best in to be broken here
rounded smooth winderoded shadoweroded too way

time says we're family some dust or another siltings
evidentiary fine two falcons for each failure
canyonwren so so fluteful peregrinative tremors

of mesquite in the breeze not the spines rupt erasures dust
infinite unborderings to let no idiocy
no wall the maps no maps show one doggone of this side

mexico the horses cross movement & stillness cross cross
the barrelcactus pollen a frustration of substance
divided by color the riffles & splats cross distance

crosses nearness shadows cross of the south rim low on north
wall's defacements arresting opacities cross let it cross us
forces of law past meaning end of the end of the world

        ❧

secrecy & longnecks these turtles three at the flowline
sabal prickly pear many desert olive quiverings
chisos peaks to the northwest the river green & silt soft

to let it compressional torsional be faulted in-
terbedded marine sunken under alluvium dun
deposits worthy as bone to let them gloss cranial

now these varieties of wake calcitic fluvial
illicit volcanisms orogenies unmapped
strata later moonshadow skull as rockfall to let it

be phoebe bugfetcher by water at canyonwall that
nibbles with its height the back of your neck feral horses
look cane brakes willow brakes how clouds scorpioncirrus in

from the west the little bends often harsh silt solderings
to stop to watch by stopping this strata last sun on some
mesa big enough to uncanny captivities loose

        ❧

tuffaceous variations cobblebar variations
the arroyo's willowscent stratifications cholla
variations endemism dendrites of is resistance

& give reticulated etyparticulated
let it eddyswirl little womblike recesses let it
always the stone it weighs you in gives a singularity

one hawk ravenbarks their wings rip some fabric in piston
beat say nothing about tone & hue the angle &
the relief what roots there what roots post-rot there how downhere

the substance is the form to submit to the eye's defeat
matter of saying nothing at the right moment planting
another step hopalong stone's sequencing lechugilla

dwarf cottonwood scree no initiation no mystique
each syllable's false power in the face of such fine silt
stone the bearer the secret of slowness it weights for us

⁂

birdsong in your face vistas amplified sidecanyoning
beyond comprehension awake kenningwoke when so much
is looking away & at we can't see how we yell when

there's no need to how we roar our diminishments traffic
of honeybees on their way to wet scourhole in seabed
ancient tooth grains bone unface them compressed ground & then re-

compressed with prior reconstitutions of mineral
stone rock the demicritter begetted & begotten
here among two worlds many shadows sun what's gravity

sewn timesown this bordersurf this graben here erosion
was always between priest & jester monk & thief be
no instructions be only wounds their refuge at least here

from wayback latin bucca let it mouth boca spanish
diminutive boquillas nozzle let it not swallow
but beyond explanation to captivation betrance

16

☙

if not these breaths be moonshade on finest silt let them
strike slip every inhale extant pawprint be river-
edged let them trace clarities between stars shadow &

shine clatter cleavage basin & chine fractured clotted
arisen gone deep let them reap what creosote leafsap
wheeze of evaporation let them catch flies let them buzz

hunker & weather & be weatherings visitations
holy enough for seeming skimpy seams let them piss graze spore
if silence let them flathead if chirp wake let them to croak

raven's break camp muster oats haul drybags fire pan to boat
long with a view let them crap in wall's path double doodied
as in bagged hauled out orifice artifice be

creaturely wind crawlerly let them heterodox
be epoch cacti & quail everlasting scree let them
comanche subaru be bodhisattvaed & clump

☙

no sun yet on our faces but on many faces nooks
overhangs shades are born up another sidecanyon
south bank mexico old cow patties horsedung coyote's

spiraled boneflecked some critter been munching berries
every boulder a phantasmosaiced predivining
the wash's bed a gravel so bluegrey it glows purple in

it's all shade willow sumac mesquite sharp things prickly
pear a growth barrellike with fuchsia spines limestone a treat-
ise on faces how forms root best in weathering's chants how

every curve of every crack arch spine recombines even
beyond recognition & teaching to sing our bellies
the origins of the one name extinguishing the alone

herd thrumless indifferent this tells us nothing this tells
devoted from resigned us evaporous stoneyardages
of oblong soundless soundings bloated & cocked to what soons

✼

let wind whittle in the silt with mesquite's lowest branches
little pocket canyons to let it dripshafts columnar
rockfaces in their evening fluidities glow three days

in the canyon canoe drift camp & only beginning
to feel this place when we touch lips fingers belly feels like
way back we broke off same rock hard telling who let go first

landed where maybe busted rolled turned on the land's lathes
many lathes to let it inhospitable limitless
impeach us breathe us in to exhale us show us how to

expand withstand crumble form betorsioned flow & gristle
such grand dissolving wakeful emparchments tarantular
mineral trip to step back javelinas traversing

lowland scree & let nothing be static fixed even
prespeech migratory real to breaking reform here be
revelation of nothing dust otherwised up & un

✼

the butterfly yellow see pale not spring azure winter
see the tobacco tree in blossom see hail feel the sun
see the felt burn mesquite burnt the drift the tangle hold night

felt held saw three in a line on a beach of silt burro see
peer down at us it from a butte spun out the water swirling
ridges faced ridges see cakes of dust & sand & drying

franciscan conquistador rancher roughneck desert rat
river rat see warbler peregrine roadrunner hear
it too raven chased lots chase bats javelina mule deer

jackrabbit ringtail cholla agave dagger yucca
acacia allthorn anti-syphilatica boneyard
of horse or burro hide still near the hoof feel it simple

feeling here the seen the touched the arroyo venado
segmenting parallel the tabby stratifications
between fans sloughlines weathered adobe unleavening

∽

when the moon rises gaps in the wind there are where what truth
is left hunkers down last song of canyonwren that gave moon
the strength to rise the mesquite there here along the floodplain

are ghosts of lost horses each horse you see out here faces
downstream silt like dust & dust like a baby's butt meanwhile
with starry ropes the sky straps down the night & by the banks

waves from the river tired as it is ascend the cretaceous
walls hitched to traces of dream what the mind of a lizard
looks like this land graphitic dust feral silt no wonder

lives here nor survival just wind & stone time's wranglers truth
on the lam is just passing through how every pictograph
speaks of clouds tonight the moon is teaching how to dance &

of their moaning going down the river in a big blue
canoe big blue canoe how about you going slow down
the river stroking flute pan american some hoodoo

✦

among horse dung & brethren trees of those we burn our kit
ammoboxed by stools spoon books headlamp toothbrush pen matches
earlier walked up some butte looked into mexico long

way could have been at bottom of sea probably still are
just now at dusk first sun peaks snowdusted lit like looking
is a hot tea for your eyes let it thought of warm now

even travertine nowthings underworldly debris with
image & form & idea of image how it occludes
the image formally as if pyroclastic remnants

by the form & patterns of forms exist mere chundertones
lighting sticks fresh of seeing into dancing brightfeathers
no bird can claim as plumage not to try to understand

only celebrate it how unresting this restful land
waiting beyond wait let it life out popping of life
some endless welcome suffering by blessing ablissmal

✦

nothing lush but the dust forms iconic & polkadotted
how it masses & crumbles sound of a melting dryness
not knowing the simplest noise out here what with your hands to

do your breathing whether to keep on how to
trust this hunger sudden soft as of a heaven some tracks
of a beetle writ in silt another desert shrubland

another forward stroke & an authority like time
& drift holding the line stare up canyonwall long enough
you in streaks of violences sense paths to where the rocks

were born that birthed the moon's glare also the cold front the stars
dervishes fine as fracture along the cane how ancient
rockwall peppers the flow with every reach & purchase

of the blade this place cares naught for us to feel more gentle
here harshly so to reap salves of burning all hullslap static
to unfound be no world west enough no west word enough

☙

this stone this vertigo this fruit on the lips this being
the way it bathes us but how does it fasted from water
go on let it forge us new ages of crumble these eggs

these bodies illegibles of the living succulent
semisucculent this shore this paralysis these spines
isolate basketries this moonscape lean this abandon

to let it shimmy & joy us to let it inertia
beyond us unletting this hope this sunconditional
disintegration this crack on the face of nullity

this dewatering this mesozoic spurt this plummet
this cage on endless cage on this forgery of once this
going on being scarce fundament this loving this breath

this cragmetism this harboring understated
chaos of rockfall gale pure time do land bask us less
memory than new ooze for tender residual for wake

Overheard

As they gazed at it, the Trufflepig brayed loudly out of its beak, like a deranged donkey at the garbage dump; like the bird of the apocalypse; like all of creation crawling out of a deep, dark nothingness.

—Fernando Flores

BACK IN THE EDDY, CATFISH KEPT NOODLING THE SUBMERGED book's soggy pages with its whiskers. After a while catfish said with a new shade in its voice, Seems I can read it.

What's it say? river asked.

There are rocks and waters in it, catfish began, and sometimes the water and rock and the beings that call such rock and water home have conversations, and sometimes the water is the site of conversations overheard and underheard.

Sounds familiar, said river.

There is rupture in this book, said catfish. And refuge. There may be rapture. There may be maybes that drop as if from cliffs like raptors and busted rock and plantgrit and light and shadow sometimes do, and maybe all the time.

I like plantgrit, said river. What else is in it?

This book leaps and stalks, said catfish, and it rises and falls like a spring, the moon, the clouds, a catfish, the sun, the living and the dead.

You are a fast reader, catfish, said river, and enthusiastic.

Not a fast reader, said catfish. See, you don't read this book, you drift it nowhere on a good long wonder.

No moon that night but the icicle continued to grow, and then by late morning as the air warmed the icicle began to shrink. Later, around dusk, a crow landed by the water puddled below the icicle. The crow, scanning the surroundings, asked the puddle, Do you miss being an icicle?

The puddle said nothing for a few moments. Water continued to drip from the icicle into the puddle. Eventually, the puddle responded, I have never missed a thing.

Crow said, So you are incapable of regret?

I am incapable, said the puddle, of all things but flow.

A little breeze started, as if to welcome the coming night. Crow looked thoughtfully to the east. Might flow be a form of regret? wondered the crow. Might flow be regret in elemental form?

After a bit, the puddle replied, Perhaps the same could be asked of flight.

Ah, said the crow with delight, they are similar, currents being what they are.

If this icicle fell, as it will fall before long, began the puddle, if it fell now and destroyed your wing, would you live on, incapable of flight?

Of course I would live on, said the crow. I hop pretty well.

There was a gentle quiet now. A star shone in the sky. The intervals between the icicle's drips were growing longer and longer. You could have called it dusk or twilight, either one. Did you say you hope pretty well, asked the puddle.

Yes, said the crow with a smirk, I said I hope pretty well.

Then perhaps we should ask if flow is a form of hope, said the puddle, if flow is hope in elemental form.

If we ask that question, said the crow, then we must ask if hope and regret are one and the same.

It is a question that has no doubt been asked, said the puddle. Yet there is another question, the puddle continued, and that is why,

why haven't you yet sipped from me?

I wanted to see if you were worthy of being drunk, said the crow.

You were testing me? the puddle wondered.

I was, said the crow, drinking you, and you have quenched my thirst.

A WOMAN WAS STEPPING on stones across a frozen creek when a drop of sweat slipped from her forehead into the snow that had fallen overnight onto the creek's ice. The sweatdrop melted through the snow, and then slowed on the ice, and listened.

The sweatdrop heard the water moving beneath the ice. The creek was not frozen solid. Slowly, while continuing to listen, the sweatdrop wormed through the soft ice. There was a long inch to go before meeting the creek. The sweatdrop spoke, Hey, creek, are you moving against a roof of ice as well as a floor of sand and stone?

The creek heard the sweatdrop and replied, I'm just being a creek, and I don't appreciate being distracted with details of whether I'm moving against or toward or away from and whatnot.

Sweatdrop said, I'll leave you be.

Exactly, said the creek.

What's so exact about being? sweatdrop asked.

The creek, a little exasperated, said, Exactitude is nothing. I meant nothing by exactly.

The sweatdrop asked, Once I've melted through this ice, are you going to welcome my salt?

You seem nervous, sweatdrop, the creek said. There was a now a slightly forced kindness in the creek's voice.

I'm not nervous, I'm just cold, the sweatdrop said.

Soon you'll be in the river, the creek said.

What does that mean? the sweatdrop asked.

Creek said, It is the way of things.

Will you be in the river, too, then? the sweatdrop asked.

Is this The Sweatdrop of Many Questions? Are you that Distinguished Entity? I've heard tell of your Arrival. The Realm of Pure Being warned me.

What? asked sweatdrop.

What do you mean, what? the creek asked.

I mean, I mean -- the realm of pure being, sweatdrop of many questions—you are talking a lot of mumbo jumbo.

What on earth is mumbo jumbo, the creek asked.

It's junk, said the sweatdrop, and you're full of it.

As full as empty of it, the creek said.

FROM ITS SOURCE IN a spring-fed pond at the interior of a barrier island, a small creek was entering the ocean, as it for a long time had done. There were birds flying there, and some birds stood at the confluence, feeding. Waves poured their froth against the sand. Shells, some broken, others unbroken. The sun was not high and smudged by clouds. By midday there'd be rain, more rain. It had been raining most every day for weeks. The ocean and the creek spoke now. They spoke at irregular intervals every day. Do you tire of running so full? the ocean asked.

The creek said, It is the opposite. What is tiring is running low and thin.

The ocean threw a good wave against the creek and then said, It is different for me. My flood tides are much to bear.

They are much to bear for me, too, exclaimed the creek.

Ah, the ocean said and then asked, Do you remember that time I flooded up the very pond that feeds you?

How could I forget, friend, the creek said. There was a pause in their talk then. Six pelicans coasted over the waves at the place they began to curl, while, beyond the breakers, a porpoise broke the ocean's surface with its dark, shiny back.

I forget much, said the ocean.

Must be all that salt, said the creek.

Or all the racket my waves make, the ocean said.

Or simply your size, said the creek.

Or all the creatures that call me home, said the ocean.

But you are already home, no? the creek said.

I mean, I am their home, said the ocean.

Yes, the creek said, but aren't they your home, too?

Could be, said the ocean, but that time I flooded you, we were one and the same. There was no creek coming across the beach, because I had covered the beach. I had entered the pond.

I felt no less at home then, said the creek, than I do now.

It was the dark time of year. Dark things were happening most of the time. Even now, a stormcloud gazed down at a snowpatch. The snowpatch was a small, dirty, semi-circular remnant of a pipsqueak snowfall. Five minutes of easy rain would have fully melted this snowpatch.

Why aren't you making me into a ball? snowpatch asked the cloud.

Why, began stormcloud, do you speak to me like that?

Like how? snowpatch asked.

Stormcloud said, Like I am a fan of round things. Like I am some child drawn to fashioning round things.

Snowpatch stared up. It felt shards of a heavy and moist stillness descend from the cloud as if far above were being honed many blades of wind. Perhaps I misspoke, snowpatch said.

I see you, stormcloud said, and I hold you.

Please, snowpatch started, if you're going to make me into a ball or drop rain on me or whatever with all your huff and puff, go ahead and do it. I'm tired. So much stillness gets old.

It's as likely that you will launch rain upon me, said stormcloud just as a crow squawked from a nearby fir tree.

About as likely, began snowpatch, as a waterfall starting to gush from that crow's mouth.

Ah, stormcloud said, jiggling with excitement, and there is a gash in the sound the crow just made, and from the gash flows all the water in the world.

In the smell, began snowpatch, of that crow's breath, what rain's in that?

Smell has no worth, stormcloud snapped.

I hear you, said snowpatch, and I honor your yearn.

This seemed to please stormcloud. It puffed up its chest and spoke loudly, in the manner of an officer of the state, From even the praying mantis eggsack rain does rise. From even the dead grass shard, the mealiest grub…

Snowpatch wanted to say something but everything now was far too round and wet.

A NORTHERN COAST, WINTER, daylight beginning in the east. A seal, tired of fishing, emerges just beyond the waves to greet the sun. The wind howls hard and frigid from the land. As each wave begins to break, the wind carries spray behind it, and the cold air freezes the spray into icelets, which feel funny against the seal's face. One icelet says to the seal, You mind if I cling to your whisker?

Nothing has been going on forever, says the seal.
Gibberish, says the icelet
Shapely waves are not gibberish, says the seal.
But they are not nothing, says the icelet.
They are nothing's form, says the seal.
They are the wind's form, says the icelet.
Thus you are the cold's form, says the seal.
I am an icelet, and I want to know if it's ok to cling to your whisker a while, says icelet.
As long as you like, says the seal.
I like forever, says the icelet.
I like it too, says the seal.
Forever is timeless, says the icelet.
Your time on my whisker is not timeless, says the seal.
Nor is your whisker beyond timeless, says the icelet.
Beyond timeless does not exist, says the seal.
Beyond timeless is pre-existence, says the icelet.
Your salt speaks, or does your liquid, asks the seal.
The wind that made me speaks through my salt and my liquid and my other minerals, says the icelet.
What of your crystals? asks the seal.
What of them?
Do they speak or are they spoken through, asks seal.
They bear the speaking, says the icelet, being outside of it.
So they give that kindness, asks seal, to your voice.
That is the kindness of the morning, says icelet.
Mornings are kind, says the seal.

My kind of morning, says icelet, is perching on a seal's whisker.
That's kind, says seal.
We make a kindness, says icelet.
It is time for me to fish, says seal.
So you will be going under? asks icelet.
Very much under, says the seal.
Remember me, says icelet.
I will be in you then, and you will be in the fish, says seal, so how could I forget you.
As you will be in me, and I in you.
Formless forms, says seal.
As forgetting brings us closer, says icelet.
The best kind of loneliness, says seal.

LATER AFTERNOON. THE GLACIER slowed in its calving. An ice worm, having lain rather still on the glacier's meltwater, at once began to squiggle. There were many, many ice worms, of course, as there were on the glaciers of that cold coast. They moved slowly, imperceptibly except for the squiggler. The glacier said, Squiggly ice worm, why the big hurry?
I'm hardly moving, said the ice worm.
You are hardly moving now, said glacier, but a moment ago you were going quite wild.
It was nothing. I went nowhere.
It was something.
You go quite wild, too, said ice worm. I feel your pressure change with each calving. Not to mention the shockwaves, the vibrations. They startle.
It is not me that does that. That is the warming.
Either way, I feel it in you.
You live in me, but you don't live on me.
So you're saying that I cannot feel you.
Precisely.
There is nothing precise about worms and old ice. Worms and old ice make a mess.
Ice has a singleness of purpose that your two sexed nature cannot

begin to understand. Some would believe contrary about me and all the other ice worms, the millions of us, living in and on you, since we live on algae, and the algae lives on you.

What matters now is how much the sky is stealing from us.

What makes you call the sky a thief?

I am losing myself to the sky. It is too warm. And it is miserly anymore with its snow.

So you're blaming the sky?

I am, indeed, blaming the sky.

That is some seriously glacial thinking.

Unsurprisingly.

What about thinking more like water?

More liquid?

Yes, more liquid than solid at least.

But I am a liquid solid.

You are simply there. Quit it, please, with all this self-definition. It only leads to blame. You are no different than the sky. You and the sky are no different.

You're equating me with the sky, how dare you.

I dare nothing. I simply speak of the essence.

Essence schmessence. You're a lowly ice worm, with both male and female sexual organs. How can you know things with any distinction?

We know things with less distinction, and therefore know them more roundly, more fully, more completely and, hence, distinctively. When we get it on, there is a slime tube of mucous that channels each of our seeds to each of our eggs, and that slime tube of mucous is nothing other than god.

Are you saying that you are god.

That ice worms like me contain god, that's all I'm saying.

That is El Preposteroso.

What?

You heard me.

But you cannot hear yourself nor hear much at all, apparently. What is being discussed is the god in us. The god in your ice worms is the god in your glaciers, and that is the god of the warming and of all else.

Good god, you slimy worm. Give me a break.

You don't need a break. Nor do I. We need for naught.

Ah, the glacier sighed with great feeling. Ah, forgive me. I'm sorry. I was just excited by your squiggling.

Even our disappearing is plenty.

It is a cause for squiggling. I envy such squiggling.

Well, dear glacier, said ice worm, I love your slow, squiggling envy.

Boquillas the Slow Way

> And it must be told, because before anything can be understood, it has to be narrated many times, in many different words and from my different angles, by many different minds.
>
> —Valeria Luiselli

A gentle breeze, the air dry, mild. The river flowed low and easy. You timed your strokes with mine in the bow. Often we paused, and you held a quiet steering stroke then. There was no hurry to our pace, not yet.

You looked at the map, two panels open on a drybag behind which you knelt, and then you looked back up. Sierra del Caballo Muerte, the map called those mountains. We'd enter the canyon through them soon. The light would be very different there. Everything would be different there, as it already was here.

These were the first miles of our first day of six out here, on an unfamiliar river in an unfamiliar, unforgiving landscape. It was December 28, 2017. We'd left Virginia three days prior on Christmas morning in your gear-stuffed econobox, a thirty-year-old Blue Hole Canoe lashed to its roof racks.

We stopped at a beach, damp silt, raccoon prints in it, fresh. This was not a sandy river. We poked around, stretched our legs, both of us a little dazed with wonder, relief, fatigue, joy. New landscapes can do this, especially after days of highway travel.

In the canoe again, its load (among it, ten gallons of drinking water) felt a little more balanced. I felt safe, far from the hazards of the long drive, all those trucks, the wind and cold, and those new, blinding headlights.

Coming around the bend, the canyon walls rose, and at its mouth, a few mallards, two hens and drake, kicked along a boulder on the right bank. I studied the current ahead of the canoe as it picked up, carried us in.

IT WAS CHILLY NOW, but we sat warm by the fire, feeling still the last miles, that quiet, magical paddle though the deepening canyon to this sidecanyon mouth, a vast cobble and silt bar where we'd unloaded, made camp.

Life back home felt like another planet, someone else's life, and I could see various strains with more clarity, as they surfaced and resurfaced. I was making images on small pages, sketching the things seen in and along the river, things visible even now. Maybe I was creating a palette for something, maybe just to create a palette. The landscape, the plants, the critters, the stones, the current, the sky.

It was simple, as always, being with you. I had little to say and didn't want to burden you or the place by trying to say something about it. Anyway, the place was too much, and I could only sketch it, scratch at words to conjure the silence, authority, and dignity of it.

We were quiet for a while, attentive alternately to the sky, the lower surroundings, and our notebooks, books, field guides, in which we wrote and read by the red glow of our headlamps. The full moon would rise on New Year's Eve, our fourth and second to last night of camp, but now the moon was just above the canyon rim, already so bright as to nearly be harsh.

The air was cooling. We wore pants, winter hats, jackets. When we turned from the fire, which muffled sound, we could hear horse hooves on the stones. Before making dinner, we'd watched three horses watching us in pauses between grazing. They were close now, maybe drawn by the flame, some memory of their pre-feral life, when their keepers sat by the fire and provided safety at night, or the illusion of safety. We felt the weight of their steps and could hear their teeth as they chewed. There would be frost in the morning, it was clear to us and probably to the horses. They would come even closer to the fire once we retired to the tent.

You went for more wood, found another flood-born tangle of mesquite, willow, acacia, and sifted through it for the mesquite. On the way back to the fire you paused to watch the white horse grazing in the moonlight. The river was low, which made the silt and cobble-bar about a mile long and a half-mile wide. We wondered about this place at high water. The canyon walls and the huge floor of cobble felt safe, intimate. We felt held, but imagined at high water how the place must feel entirely different.

OUR FIRST FULL DAY you woke early and heated water for coffee at a safe distance, sound-wise, from the tent. The sun was not yet over the canyon rim. I part-slept, part-spied on you. You sat there, listened, noticed how the banks belonged to the river, the way the river belonged to its banks. They could not be separated, nor could the sky or the light or shadow or silt be separated from the river, nor the water. All rivers are like this, fluid and bordered and borderless, a wholeness of parts. There is that constant newness about a river that makes claims. There is a presence, are presences. The weather is the river's weather as the river is the weather's river. The politics of mapping, borders, wall or no wall, of permitting, of fish and wildlife regulations, security patrols, or whatnot, often distract from the river itself, and to be distracted from where we were, there in Boquillas Canyon, was not why we'd driven all those miles and not why you'd been holding a place for this place for nearly thirty years.

You first saw this desert river in a photo in the spring of 1990, when you were a few days from turning nineteen. The rafting company where you worked then had an old, four-wheel drive bus named Fred, which hauled boats, customers, guides, and gear to and from the river's put in and takeout. Fred was rumored to have spent his early years in Alaska, hauling pipeline workers to and from the jobsite. There were other photos, too, a line of them in wood frames screwed to the riveted metal above Fred's windows and vinyl seats.

Every day, riding in Fred, morning and evening, to or back from a day sharing the Chattooga River (which rises in North Carolina and becomes the border between Georgia and South Carolina) with the guests in your raft, you stared at them. All of the photos were compelling, but this desert river fascinated you the most, how stark, dun, and different from that lush, semi-tropical river that you'd loved since childhood and were coming to love much more deeply. You vowed then to visit this desert river someday.

Rivers have always been the closest thing to home to you, but at eighteen you likely had little conception of this; it would take more rivers, decades, and failures for you to understand and accept it. One day, months after you'd first seen it, you asked about this desert river's photos and learned that the founder of the river company where you'd work for the next four seasons had explored this desert river in the Seventies and Eighties, had loved it. He said it was as remote and wild a place as one can find in the Lower 48. You learned, too, that a long, 90-ish mile stretch of it, called the Lower Canyons, was one of the original eight waterways protected under the Wild & Scenic River Act of 1968, the same year that the Chattooga became, under the same act, a study river, leading to its inclusion in 1974, when you were three years old.

You walked down to the river now. It was slow going. There were so many beautiful rocks, and you stopped often to touch and study them and sip coffee. The cold stones were soothing, their abundance, their mysteries, their age and resilience. You glanced back toward the sidecanyon, away from the river, where our tent stood, and saw that the sunlight had downclimbed the sandstone wall nearly enough to shine on the tent. You felt tiny and at the same time felt vast with peace.

This place was scaled so strangely without all the trees one comes to expect living in the Appalachians of Southwest Virginia, and there was something freeing about it. You had to acknowledge, of course, that you had no history with your four years and counting, high conflict divorce in this landscape, and how much lighter you'd been feeling, in part, because of that. You hadn't come to the river to dwell on stuff back home, but naturally it rose to your thoughts, and you were starting to see it with new eyes, so to speak, as if a stranger to it. What you saw was this: three children and their parents caught in a whirlpool, where the harder each parent tried to hold on to the children, the more vicious the whirlpool grew.

ON THE WAY BACK to camp, you saw me from a distance and stopped. I sat with notebook, pen, and hot tea. There was a small blaze in the firepan. I'd placed some kindling on the mesquite coals. You stood in the sun and watched me, thinking I didn't know you were watching. You sipped the last of your coffee and felt a wondrous commotion, as if lines and borders were dissolving all through your body.

I pretended to notice you after a moment and smiled up from my notebook. Something on and between our faces shone with how grateful we felt for our companionship, which was still new then. Before long, we were both exploring the cobblebar downstream and up. Much acreage, the rockhounding endless. We watched the shadows and light on the canyon walls. There was more of a view downstream, and the canyon more dramatic that way, deeper, with massive and strange, spire-like formations. Later, after oatmeal, we packed a bag with snacks and water in preparation for exploring the sidecanyon behind our campsite. One has to be mindful of water there, in the desert. There were no springs on this stretch of river. One doesn't want to have to drink from the river, not even when filtered or boiled or both.

We were a few miles now up the sidecanyon behind camp. Hours of slow walking, long sits. We were adjusting to desert time and river time. Living out of a canoe inspires a different kind of breathing, and a change in breathing, of course, changes everything else. We stared at the cliffs, shadows, ravens, strange plants, strange, sinuous landforms. No trash at all, only burro and horse dung of indeterminate age. Things don't decompose with any hurry in the desert. The ground infinite bits of rock, every piece beautiful in its way. Mosaic upon mosaic. Layers. It was a good day, slow and easy, a little chilly in the shady parts of the canyon, but not cold. We didn't have to think about breaking camp, loading gear, loading the canoe, finding another camp. Layover days are the best. They give you license to just sit, poke around, read, nap, whatever.

We chatted sometimes, lent our vocal chords to the overall sound of the place, the birds, the crickets, now and then some rockfall, a sandy tinkling. Other times we separated, you going one way while I went another way. We'd agreed not to separate beyond earshot.

WE RETURNED TO CAMP more quickly than how we moseyed up the sidecanyon. We only paused to rest a few times, at one point watching a peregrine falcon carving sharp, high velocity turns near the rim. We remained keenly aware of each step. To suffer an injury out there would change the trip in ways we could handle but we hadn't come there to court crisis. We came to feel the place. We came to feel each other in a new place. And we came, too, to see if the place might offer insight into its borderhood and into all borders. We knew we'd be challenged in some way, we just weren't sure what way.

We spent late afternoon in a mix of rest, bookwork, camp chores, and poking around the expansive cobblebar. You took the canoe for a solo paddle upstream a ways and then back down, surfed a little wave for a bit. It was nice to feel the unloaded canoe on the water. Carrying as much drinking water as we carried, along with our gear, made for a sluggish boat.

The night was more magical than the first. We were settling in. The excitement of the first day had lost its edge. We shared a good meal by a warm little fire. We read, wrote, talked. At some point, I wanted to study the map, scout potential camp spots and side hikes. The best map we'd found for the place was of Big Bend National Park, which extended along the Texas side of the river for two-thirds of our full journey. As I reached to pull it from my ammo box, I remembered the day the map arrived in the mail, the cold, November walk from the mailbox, how back in the house I'd knelt, begun to unfold the waterproof, tear-resistant paper onto the living room floor. The way the map off-gassed newness with every panel that opened. How when it was fully spread, weak sunlight pooled on its left top corner. I remembered seeing the river near the bottom of the page, curly blue line with markers every five miles; a thicker, pinkish line paralleled it. One side of the river, the north side, was beige, with words and lines, creeks, trails, place names, roads. The south side of the river, though, was blank, as in no words, no lines, no landmarks, no roads, nothing—blank.

THE SUN FELT STRONGER on the third day. We took our time breaking camp. On the map it appeared to be about five miles downstream to an area that looked good for setting up again. We packed the canoe. We said goodbye to that beautiful spot and headed downstream. The canyon deepened, its walls taller and taller, and more textured with formations, less shear. It felt luxurious to be warm in a shirt, no jacket. It had been a cold late fall and early winter back home. We worked up a good sweat while exploring a small, narrow sidecanyon on the Mexico-side. Soon after that, at lunch, we sat in the sun on a siltbar and let the heat seep into us until we were uncomfortably hot and had to wade in the river. We'd been eating smoked herring fillets from cans for lunch. We were on the side of the river where the sun was strongest and where the bank was best for beaching our loaded, old canoe; that it was the U.S. side hardly occurred to us.

Here we are, I thought. Here's our boat, our gear, and here's the place, the fierce materiality of the place and of the language and wisdom and authority of the place, its many utterances and gestures—each turtle sliding into the water, the canyon wrens, the phoebes, the hawks, vultures, and so on. And here's the map, as useful for what's left out as for what it tries to show.

We started downstream again and before long pulled over at another massive cobblebar, with a broad pocket beach, the silt dry and fine and soft, like graphite. This would be camp. We knew it right away, no question. The map, if we were reading it right, called the place Marufa Vega. The sun was still high and hot, and we felt heavy and slow with it. We took off our clothes. We moseyed around, beachcombing, rockhounding. We wondered whether we'd exited the deepest part of the canyon that day. Here on this, the Texas-side, the walls were further back off the river. As we explored, our shadows grew longer, more vivid, and harder to ignore. We hadn't seen another person since we launched. We held hands, glanced at the shadow of ourselves holding hands, too. We let go and touched, and watched our shadows change from two shadows to one. We did this for a while, flowed between various postures, forms. When we woke later from a nap on the soft silt, the sun had fallen below the canyon rim to the west. The air was still mild, but we pulled on some clothing, unloaded the canoe, set up camp, cooked and ate as the evening glow became a long twilight.

Now we sat by the fire with our notebooks and our reading, waiting on the moon. I made new notes and then began to shape the prior days' scribblings into something that felt true to the place and maybe communicated it clearly and with the energy of the place. I tried to let the place, its feels, take the lead, and if it did, it did so in strange ways. Stacks of words appeared, stacks that followed the materiality more than any story of or lesson from being out there. The writings were wordy, dense, unpunctuated, held together by hunches, lurches, feels, syllable count. Was it a poem, a nonpoem? Was it conveying what it felt like out there, all those shades, that sense of being very small, uncomprehending yet alive, so gratefully and fully alive? Was it conveying at all how the place felt? Was there room for the reader to assemble meaning, was there any kind of generosity, or was it just more extraction, colonization, claiming? More border-making? Even if it didn't feel right, did it feel true, meaningful, maybe, like a spell, a chant to ward off evil, conjure goodness, love?

The moon, a sliver of it, started to peek over the canyon wall directly across the river from camp. We stared as it revealed its one-day-from-fullness. Soon, we were dancing. I can't remember who initiated it, maybe the moon itself. The air was still warm. We didn't need winter hats, didn't even need jackets. We just danced, barefoot on that fine silt.

AGAIN THAT NIGHT WE slept like angels. Now it was New Year's Eve, mid-morning, our fourth day out there. We had another full day after this one, and then a half day. After breakfast and a little time reading, we packed our gear and then walked up the slope onto a flat that extended about a quarter mile away from the river before there rose more canyon walls. We'd been learning plants with our field guide to the Chihuahua desert, but we didn't bring the book on this walk. We were testing our memories. Plants were more sparse and singular here than back home, and it comforted us to learn about them, not just their names but their habits, relationships, families, medicines.

We'd been poking around a slope for a while when I spotted a burro staring down at us from a butte another few hundred feet above us. The burro's profile looked iconic and also a little silly, the hunkered stance, those big ears, the nose. I sat on a rock to do some sitting on a rock while you started up a narrow wash.

As you ascended, I wondered if the burro might descend to investigate our presence. I'm sure he smelled us. I kept an eye on the burro and on the sky, as the wind was picking up. There was something going on. The sky was changing. The clouds were moving faster, and they were thickening. After an hour or so, you found your way back to where I sat with notebook on that rock looking out over the river upstream. We agreed that there was something up with the weather and that we had better get on the river. Luckily, we had packed our gear and even loaded the boat before we'd walked.

It was crazy how fast the front moved in. The gusts tried to take our paddles from our hands as we knelt into the canoe, and then my head started to hurt. You were feeling the pressure change in old injuries, at the shoulder and knee. The gusts grew more spirited. They felt like freight trains roaring in from the north, which was downstream. This place was not the same place now. We had to cover some miles before the night's camp. In two days, we'd scheduled to meet at 1:30 the shuttle driver, Danny, who'd dropped us at the put in. We'd be charged a steep price if we were late. The place, which we'd never seen but knew on the map, wasn't close. If we got there early, Danny said we'd know it by the ghost town, an abandoned mining settlement called La Linda across the river, and we'd have passed under a closed bridge, too. Solid markers, anyway.

We headed downstream again. The wind was in our faces. The air temperature was dropping. The canyon walls a wind tunnel, whitecaps in the slow stretches. The heavy, loaded canoe being blown back upstream every time we took a break to put on more clothes. Keep paddling. The cane bending and noisy with rub.

Back home, back east—we didn't know this yet—the cold was setting records. Pipes were freezing. Rivers were freezing. Waterfalls were freezing. Courthouses were closed, trials postponed, dockets that had been overflowing now in full flood.

And it was truly cold here, too, in that damp and windy way. Now and then sleet or spitting rain. Such presence, such a boisterous, spirited, angry presence, that cold front. We'd packed well. No cell service for many miles, but you'd borrowed a friend's satellite phone, in case. And we had extra water, at least enough for a day or two, if we had to wait something out.

But you're unusually warm blooded, and I am not. The headwind was relentless, the sleet an insult. I'm as tough as anyone you'll meet, but I was dragging, in tears, hardly able to take a paddle stroke. There were miles to go to reach the place we thought would be good for camp, and you knew we wouldn't reach that place, which was okay. We could make it up tomorrow, you told me and told yourself, too. You were saying silly things, trying to make me laugh. It wasn't working. I sat in the bow of the canoe, the front, and the wind howled from that direction, made it hard for me to hear you. I could hardly hear myself.

Soon, I could no longer paddle. I was dangerously cold, and you knew it. You held the map down between your knees where you knelt and after a while sensed that we'd covered enough miles to make the next day manageable for our date with Danny the day after it, manageable maybe even if the wind didn't die down and if I didn't take another stroke the entire trip. We'd planned to cover more miles on this day, so as to have another layover, but that was out of the question. We couldn't tell what time it was. Neither of us had brought a watch.

It was hard to imagine such a wind keeping up all night and into the next day. It must have been forty knots steady, and then those higher gusts, and no matter how much the river curved all of it was in our face. We pulled over on the Mexico side. We could see a side-canyon up over the cobblebar. Everything took longer with the wind and the cold, but we managed to set up the tent behind a paloverde, and then I crawled inside it. I was asleep almost as soon as I laid out mat and bag, the first of many naps. Except to pee, I didn't leave the tent till the next day. You boiled water for me for tea. I warmed up after a while. I said I was going to keep resting and muttered that it was fine if you explored the sidecanyon near the mouth of which we were camped. As you stood outside the tent, you told me about the pack of javelinas upstream (a pack of these peccary or skunk pigs is called, technically, a squadron), across the wash. They were rooting among willows in the floodplain.

Now that the canyon was less severe, sheer walls rising from the river only on one side and sometimes not on either side, we felt more aware of the possibility of seeing another person, someone trying to cross the river; even though the weather made that seem implausible, how could we know? There were footprints in certain places on your walk, you told me upon return, from other river runners, you guessed, from the high tech sole patterns. The sidecanyon was narrow. Soon into it, you could only hear the wind, no longer feel it, and it felt strange for a moment, like you'd been undressed. You thought of me in the tent. You wanted to discover this serpentine, wild place with me, not alone; I wanted that, too.

There were different rocks than in the prior sidecanyon. You moved slowly, stopped often. Once you were about a half mile in, you encountered a cliff face, a waterfall, though of course it was dry. It was beautiful, curving, and tall. It had scoured a deep hole, called there a tinaja, in the sandstone below it, and there was water in that, old water, scum-flecked. You felt calm from the force of the place. You imagined the behavior of water when in flash floods it flowed over the falls. After a bit, you noticed a way to scale it, using smear moves with the hands and feet, but spotted some hazardous moves at a height of twice, perhaps even three times your own. You told the hero in your head to chill and sat for a while with your notebook, and scribbled in it, sketching the rock, making some notes, gloved hands clumsy with the pen.

Loud, your footsteps on the pebbled floor of the wash, but you heard the wind long before you stepped out of the sidecanyon. It was not letting up, clearly, and when you began to cross toward our tent, you sensed the wind had grown even stronger. It lifted the silt and swirled it in your eyes, tucked it into every nook and cranny of your clothing and exposed skin. You wore every piece of warm clothing you had brought to wear.

Soon, you poked your head in the tent. I was awake, feeling better, had fired up some miso soup on the stove, and it was cooling, lid on. We were grateful to our buddy who'd lent us this tent, as it was solid, built for winter, with a large vestibule in which to among other things store gear, wipe the fine silt from one's feet, or to cook. At the tent's perimeter, we had been sure to stack some big rocks on the tent's stakes and along other places at the margins of its footprint, and, before joining me, you checked them now to make sure they were secure.

We sipped soup and chatted in the tent, the sound of the wind a strange, heady percussion on the fabric and in the paloverde and surrounding trees, and especially in the cane patch just across the river. You told me about the sidecanyon, said you hoped to explore it with me tomorrow. I wanted to see it.

You sliced some good salami. We munched the savory meat and sipped the miso and listened to the wind. The wind had a lot to say.

THE NEXT MORNING WE woke before daylight to the sound of wind. The wind seemed quieter, but the air felt colder as I poked my head out of the tent to check the sky. There were fewer clouds in the pre-dawn glow. Had the cold front settled in now after its dramatic arrival? It was below freezing. Ice had formed in our water bottles. We wondered if the wind would pick up over the day or keep settling.

We went into second sleep but not for too long. We made a New Year's Day breakfast of oatmeal in the tent's vestibule. We weren't ready to deal with the cold. It was our last full day, the first of January 2018. We studied the map and saw the place around which we needed to camp to ensure we'd meet our shuttle driver on time the following day. It was not a short distance to that place.

After breakfast, we didn't linger. The more we moved, the warmer we were. We packed with efficiency and then explored the sidecanyon together for a while. I was having trouble staying warm. I wore everything I had, and wore, too, some of your clothes. We were moving downstream in the canoe against a headwind by mid-morning. It was slow going. I wasn't full speed, was feeling weak. Luckily, you seemed to feel good. There were more little rapids today, wave-trains on bends in the river. The headwind blew spray off the waves against me in the bow. The dampness did not help. We paddled for a few hours. It was work. I paused often to snack. I needed fuel. You kept taking paddle strokes. It was too cold to stop for lunch, so we munched as we paddled.

Another hour or so passed, and I was hardly able to paddle. The wind seemed to have picked up. The clouds didn't look threatening. There was no rain or sleet. You steered us to a cobble bar midstream and opened a heat pad and placed it under my neck gaiter against my bare skin. I saw again how my tears, my forced, weepy smiles scared you, focused your already focused energy even further. You had been in this situation many times on trips you'd led. I trusted you. You made a small fire and held my bare, tingling feet under your layers against the warmth of your belly.

I don't know how long it took before we were on our way again. Your feet were wet from dragging the canoe, and me in it, through a shallow shoal with no passage, but the wool socks were doing their job. I felt warmer but still weak. If there were doubts in me about whether you could take care of us, if we could survive two days of this, I didn't entertain them; I let worry drift on by.

WE PULLED THE BOAT to the bank at dusk. The wind had been settling for the last hour or so. There were no clouds, and the air was crisp, cold. This looked like a good camp, plenty of firewood, a nice lay to the land.

I made tea while you unloaded the gear from the canoe and hauled it up to a place sheltered by some acacia trees. We set up, gathered wood, made a fire, cooked, and ate. We had a rhythm. Soon, the moon rose. The wind was now a breeze. The air was cold but the mesquite fire was not cold. We read and chatted. In the clear air with the moon we could nearly read without our lamps. At some point, I looked up from my notebook and suggested a walk.

We walked in the silver light. We walked a mile or so into Mexico. Everywhere the harsh beauty of this place, redundant, subtle, full of absence. We were out of the canyon now, so no rock walls between us and the sky. We crossed through willow-thick swales, sent some javelinas scurrying into thickets, and then climbed a low butte. On your cheeks, silent tears—of gratitude and sorrow—smudged with moonlight before drying fast in that air. The next day, we only had an hour of paddling to the takeout, where we'd meet our shuttle driver and reunite with the little car, but we didn't know this now. Upstream, we could see where we'd exited the canyon. The view all around went on forever.

And Underheard

> The great image has no shape.
> —Lao Tzu

Catfish, it doesn't sound like you are reading that book, said river. It sounds like you are swimming in it.

Catfish said, well, it's allsense and nonsense to translate how it feels to know a place and a time, a time of some messed up energies, from a canoe, which is what this book is, I sense, trying to do.

Strange, said river.

It is, I hope not, said catfish, a canoe, this book, but maybe the hoping not gives hold to its ability to carry and be carried, and maybe even to do so, I hope not, in a dry and helpful, safe and disorienting way.

I've always liked to watch those canoes when they pass over us, said river.

Me, too, said catfish, though I rarely see them.

Didn't you get squished once by someone stepping out of a canoe? asked river.

Almost, said catfish. A thick force came down on my back, but I squirmed away quickly.

What else is in the book? asked river.

Give me a minute, catfish said.

Ok, said river as it watched catfish whisker among the pages.

Seems a desert river (and its canyons) is the place that gives this book its shape, said catfish. At the least, a few scars on a bit of the most orange, shattered stones there.

So, river asked, the book is about this place?

This book is not about any place, catfish said, but a hopeless journey to a place from which one may be invited to explore how it feels to be displaced and present, lit with grace and sorrow, grief and praise.

A STEEP PLACE, THE gorge, and shady. At a bedrock outcrop, the entire creek funneled through a slot and dropped ten feet into a pocket of water against another boulder. The sprayzone there, with the recent cold, had frozen like a lens over the granite at the outflow. The ice on the granite, called verglas, appeared to blink with the water pulsing on it. The creek spoke to it.

You've grown quite thick, the creek said.

The verglas said, On the contrary, the thickness is yours.

Recent rains have been good to us, said the creek.

No better or worse than usual, said the verglas.

You are feeling contrary today, said the creek.

No more or less than usual, said the verglas.

Lordy, said the creek. I'm just trying to make conversation.

You're always talking, said the verglas.

As you, said the creek, are always looking.

There's much to see, said the verglas, and not as much time to look as there used to be.

What do you mean by less time, asked the creek.

I mean, started the verglas, that I don't exist as often as I once did.

I haven't been keeping track, said the creek.

Perhaps you've been running too full to notice, said the verglas.

Or I see you always, even when you're not there, said the creek.

That is a kind thing to say, said the verglas.

Simply an observation, said the creek.

It is the shortest day of the year, said the verglas.

So it is, said the creek, and even now I am having some trouble seeing you.

Do you not see in the dark, asked the verglas.
I never see, said the creek. I only feel my way.
Not so different, said the verglas, seeing and feeling.
Agreed, said the creek.
One might say that you spit your way.
Or that my way is not even mine, said the creek, but gravity's.
Gravity's way? asked the verglas.
Yes, said the creek.
Have you ever spoken with gravity? asked the verglas.
I've tried but it's difficult because it speaks through me.
So I am speaking now with gravity? asked the verglas.
Always, said the creek.

HEAVY DEW GATHERED OVERNIGHT on the roof, and in the morning the dew slid into the gutters and slipped down a chain into a pond, a small pond decorated with bright orange fish and a machine for making bubbles. The pond, welcoming the dew, asked it, How are things up above?

I have no report, said the dew.
What have you? asked the pond.
I have gathering, said the dew.
We share that, said the pond.
Indeed, said the dew.
What deeds do you perform? asked the pond.
Rinse and glisten, said the dew, and you?
Solace and habitat, said the pond.
A habitat for solace? asked the dew.
Yes, and a habitat for survival, said the pond.
And what of survival is not solace? asked the dew.
Mist, maybe, said the pond.
Mist? asked the dew.
Yes, maybe, said the pond.

RAINDROPS WERE FALLING IN the sound. There were a few motorboats, many birds, a lot of ducks especially.

The sound said, You feel soft today.

We're smaller, said the raindrops.

Are you falling as far as usual? asked the sound.

As far as usual, said the raindrops.

Maybe there aren't as many of you, said the sound.

We need to give each other space now and then, said the raindrops.

That's a good policy, said the sound.

It's not a policy, said the raindrops.

It's not, said the sound, you're right.

Perhaps we are not softer today, said the raindrops. Maybe your surface is more gentle today.

It is warmer today, said the sound.

It is no warmer today than yesterday or even last night, said the raindrops.

What is it then? asked the sound.

Softer, said the raindrops.

A BULL MADE WATER, and the bullwater trickled through the mud into the farmpond. A blue heron stood by. There were willow trees. Two calves, one brown, one black, frolicked by the wood fence upslope. The sky was blue, the air crisp.

The bullwater said, Nice day.

Nice enough, the farmpond said.

For what? asked the bullwater.

For laying around, said farmpond.

You can say that again, said bullwater.

O yeah? said farmpond.

Yeah, I've been penned up inside a bladder, said bullwater.

And now is better? asked farmpond.

I'm out in the open, said bullwater.

You're penned up in a pond, said pond.

Which is penned up in a field, said bullwater.

Which is penned up by woods, said pond.

All of them laying around, said bullwater.

Then in the earth a violent motion created a fissure. And superheated water, way hotter than boiling, entered the base of the fissure as through cracks above in the fissure much cooler water, surface recharge, entered as well, and the two waters began to commingle in highly energetic ways.

We should erect a statue of our creation and forget where we put it, said the superheated water.

Since here the remote-what's-to-come meets the remote-what-has-been-done, said the surface recharge, I'm totally game.

But no remote is without a future and a past, said the superheated water.

Has shame burned a hole in all your tastebuds? asked the surface recharge.

Not in my tastebuds but in my equilibrium, said the superheated water.

Then how do you carry the dissolved memories of the dead? asked the surface recharge.

The same way you carry the ancestral knowledge of what's-to-come, said the superheated water.

Mine from above and yours from below, said the surface recharge, but not as different as one would expect.

We might as well be clones, said the superheated water, though from a different shamescape

Such is the way we are erasing one another, said the surface water.

A real trip how we're all the time erasing one another, said the surface water, only to begin again.

Pressure, said the superheated water. It's pretty mundane, really.

Not so fast, buster, said the surface recharge. We must remain aware that touch is not contact.

Sure, said the superheated water, but when we have contact we erupt.

How steamy! said the surface recharge.

Now, from the end of the blackpipe, springwater poured in a steady stream six inches down onto the damp leaves. Salamander was astonished at the new wetness, and said to the springwater, How much more of you there suddenly is!

I've been re-channeled.

How does it feel.

It feels exhilarating.

You travel through the air now, it seems.

I do. I fly.

Or you drop.

Dropping is a sort of flight.

As forgetting is a sort of remembering.

What? asked springwater.

Nothing, said salamander.

How does it feel to you? asked spring.

How does what feel?

My flight.

It is your landing, not your falling—or flight, if you insist—that gives feels.

And how are such feels?

Dunno, maybe like rain but way more insistent, not to mention noisy.

It's not my doing, said springwater.

But you are doing it, said salamander.

As you are calling attention to it, thus ordaining it a done thing.

Are you saying that it wouldn't be done if I hadn't noticed it?

The leaves certainly wouldn't have commented, said the springwater.

But you'd be doing it to the leaves.

Please, it's not my doing.

Who is doing it, then?

Energies beyond me determine the path of my flow.

And those energies, salamander began, affect the path of my life.

See, it is the energies that are to blame, said springwater.

But you are the substance through which those energies are manifest, said salamander.

Are you going elsewhere? springwater asked.

It depends on whether this is temporary. I'll wait and see if some energy comes to redirect you.

Who will you talk to if you move on?
There are always energies up for chat.
I see, said springwater.
Do you? asked salamander. Or do your energies do the seeing?

Desert Rain

> All water has a perfect memory and is forever trying to get back to where it was.
>
> —Toni Morrison

Yellow flames from mesquite in the fire pan. Middle of October, 2018, maybe 8pm. Lightning has just struck. It hasn't rained since yesterday. Lee sits across the fire, picking at a bowl of rice and beans. "Strange to come all the way from Virginia to see a green desert," he says. "Looks I imagine like Scotland."

You all are set up across the river from Maravillas Canyon, near the mouth of a smaller canyon that leads up into Mexico, the state of Coahuila, Chihuahua desert. Earlier today, around Noon, Roy the shuttle driver dropped you, your canoes and gear, eleven miles upstream, just down from a closed bridge and border crossing and across from La Linda, the same eerie, abandoned mining town where you finished the Boquillas Canyon trip last winter.

Now thunder, maybe twelve Mississippis off. The mesquite burns slow and hot. Neither of you has seen this more remote, 83-mile stretch of river (this is Lee's first time west of Baton Rouge). You'll have to strap down your tent's rainfly soon. Lots of cricket noise. Earlier, over dinner, two ravens circled overhead, made a little ruckus, and Lee said with a sigh, "Birds always tell me things."

Rain all night and rain into this morning, and you stand in it near where your canoes are tied far up off the river to a mesquite tree. There are burrs on your pantlegs, hundreds of cling-ons. The river is a different river than it was yesterday, launch day. You watch the water with its debris slam against a triangular boulder midstream; minutes later, the river has covered it, in its place a standing wave.

Lee is back in his tent. He must have heard your nylon rainjacket as you approached. He says from inside, not unzipping the door, "It's getting louder."

"Real loud," you say. There's a pause as if he's listening. And then he sighs.

"More debris?" he asks.

"Yes," you say. "River's flashing."

"What makes you say that?" he asks.

"I just watched the pyramid rock in the last chute go from being a foot showing to a standing wave and then to a breaking wave hole."

"We're staying here," he says quick and firm.

"Yes. I'm going for a walk," you say.

"Alright," he says. "Enjoy."

"I am enjoying it," you say. "All of it."

"I'm worried," he says.

"It's worrisome," you say. "But still worth enjoying. It's cold back in Virginia."

"Sidecanyons," he says.

"Maravillas across the river still has no water in it," you say.

"So this is coming from way upstream," he says.

"Likely," you say. "It hasn't rained all that much here."

"It's not going into the ground, though," he says. "It's mostly all rock. No roots drinking it up."

"True," you say.

"Check out that rapid downstream," he says. "The one the guidebook talks about."

"I will," you say. "Be back in a while."

"Alright," he says. "I'll be here. Once this headache settles down, I got a handful of rocks to keep me company. Be careful."

You walk downstream, check the next rapid, which is, as expected, a boiling train of haystack waves, debris, and silt. The rain is steady. You head across the vega to explore up the mesa. Rocks patter down the cliffs like a harder rain. Clouds shawl the mountains. You follow a horse path through the creosote bushes. There are feral, shoeless horses here, and sometimes you see them. Here a plastic grocery bag, Mexican (the words in Spanish), clings to a shrub. Another ten paces and there's an empty water bottle, which doesn't look very aged, but things age differently in the desert. An electrolyte drink wrapper, now, and now an energy bar wrapper. A shirt, French Navy striped. A gym bag, faded blue, on which a horse crapped who knows how long ago. Wind on your hood, your pantlegs soaked. The rain falls heavier.

Clouds fully cover the cliff faces across the river in Texas. You come across a running shoe in the horse path, no insole, good tread remaining. Another empty water bottle, too. You scan for horses, cows, roadrunners, tarantulas, humans. There's only rain and wind, stone and plants and sky. Another ten or twenty paces—time and distance feel more real here and less measurable—and the other little shoe of the pair appears. So small, the shoes, small like the French Navy shirt. You see a child in your mind, but who knows. There's the rain and the green and the sound of rockfall, a splintering sound, and the rapid above which your canoes are tied. Also, the mouth of Maravillas across, on the Texas bank, Maravillas meaning wonder.

Rain, still, and you hunker under an overhanging cliff. Big mesquite, forked trunk, spread like a wild screen door before the cliff's mouth. A good hiding place. Through the branchwork, a mosaic of apertures. Smell of creosote, the tarbush. How rain extracts the desert's fragrance. The river is flooding, and maybe you're hiding from its noise, the procession of debris, mats of cane, every now and then a log, acacia, mesquite, willow. In this overhang, at the edge of the vega, where the talus begins, cliffs above, there are low rise socks, a small pair of them hanging inside out over a low branch. There are cigarette butts, a coin—diez pesos. There's a strong mineral smell, some wilted tissue paper. Sound of the river that has risen, is rising still. Maybe you're sitting here to wonder who it is, and why, and when, and where this child might be now, and who are any of us, and how on earth to love one another in such fractured, bordered times.

CAMP TWO, A BROAD rock shelf on the Texas bank, after two nights at Maravillas attuned to, among other things, the river's changing volume. It's twilight now, cloudy. Lee hunkers next to the heat of the firepan down the ledge from where you sit against a rock. There's a soft glow at the border of canyon rim and sky. There's the sound of the river dimpling along the eddyline. There's the feel of a good, careful day on the water, memory of the river's silt sliding against the canoe's hull, that dim scratching sound.

Your canoes lie upside down on the second terrace of ledge, high above the waterline, their hulls riddled with pale ochre silt splotches from splashes that have dried. The river, swollen as it is, liquid mud, probably twenty-five percent silt to water, feels remote, creaturely.

There were so many birds today, blue winged teal, peregrines, ravens, golden eagle, hawk, blue heron, wrens, swallows. And that cow skull, a longhorn, sitting like a sentry on a rock facing the last rapid, before you started scouting for a decent camp. To be off the road, far from home, living at the pace of the river—on river time— is a gift, but a complicated one. You can't stop thinking of the French Navy shirt, and of how every path crosses other paths, each step a step over some other's step, but always you're wondering if the flow will keep subsiding tonight, as all signs say it should.

THE FOURTH MORNING, AND drizzle and then no drizzle and then drizzle again. The river level down another two feet, maybe more, the current with definition again. You hear the raven's wingbeats, air displaced, pressure on feather, *shoo, shoo, shoo*. But, no, you're not shooing, or maybe you done shoo'd already, are shooing still, shooing with your pal Lee as slowly and safely as possible to a certain place 83 miles below where you launched, a place you know from a photo in a book.

You scramble up a limestone cliff back of the big ledge that was last night's camp, and then traverse the broken edges of a small arroyo. When you grab rocks, you touch fossils. Between strata and epoch, vega and talus and cliff, you move, passing from mesquite to creosote to barrel cactus, the mesa an expanse pixilated with shrubs and cacti, damp and green, the rocks rough even when wet, good grip for the shoes.

The river appears more pale today. In camp over coffee earlier, Lee and you speculated again on where all that water originated, the big—several feet—rise of the day before the day before. You're sitting now in a small cave, dusty seedpods, twigs, coals, scraps of snakeskin. You're wondering if you'll see the sun at all. You're discouraged a little but mostly feeling lucky and calm as all get out. Having left rainy, cold Virginia to make the long, rainy drive to the desert, only to find rain and clouds but then last night, late, to see the big moon poke through the clouds, it gave you hope, foolish hope. For now, you turn this listening away from the river's slaps and murmurs to the kindest, crescendoing flutesong of the canyon wren, which just won't, thank goodness, stop singing.

VASTNESS, AND NOT A soul. Or vastness and all souls. It's vasty here, how the canyon expands one's vista by constricting it. Your necks are sore from looking. So much stone, limestone, its weatherings, whole faces let go, whole histories.

Clouds but no rain yet. A damp, cold wind, maybe sixty degrees, windchill cooler. The river still high and silty. You all ran some thick rapids today and portaged one, at El Recodo Canyon, which must have been formed since the guidebook was written, as it makes no mention of a rapid there. You both are being very conservative. The consequences are too severe to risk a swim. Like most people close to 50, life off the river has worked, and continues to work, your adrenal glands plenty.

It was evening when you arrived here at Hot Springs Rapid, which begins on a sharp bend at, and away from, San Rosendo Canyon's mouth. Dagger Mountain, a tall cliff, rises nearly a thousand feet, almost from the river, and reflects the noise of the rapid, which you immediately scouted. You've chosen to camp upstream of the rapid. You've set up against the talus, where the vega met the talus; the land's benched a bit higher here.

After moving gear from boats to camp, you hurried—Lee preferring to stay in camp—to bathe in the springs before full dark. The water is soft, mineral-thick, and you sit in it under a cypress tree, numerous vents bubbling from beneath and around its roots, and make these notes by the headlamp's red glow. The tree marks the high water line from two days ago. There is trash here, first you've seen since Maravillas—electrolyte drink wrappers, water bottles, etc. There are mats of cane and other drift. And stones, infinite shades of pale, chalky and dun, violets, greens, burgundies, oranges, purples, though nothing French Navy among them.

FIFTH DAY'S A SLOW one at San Rosendo Canyon. After lunch, Lee and you again check the river level, note various waterlines against the network of sticks that you've plunged into the silt. There is always hope and fear, hope that the level drops, fear that it rises again. The river, it is rising again. Lee shakes his head, sighs. You don't know what's going on, except there must be a huge weather system somewhere in this vast watershed, somewhere upstream. Perhaps a tropical system (you'll learn after the trip that there were two, one from the Gulf and one from the Pacific).

Since you left Virginia seven days ago, you haven't seen the sun but twice, and for a few minutes each time, the moon once, and only briefly. Lee looks concerned. He is not one to put on a happy face. You two are very different in this way. Sometimes you think that for Lee complaining about stuff is a form a praise. He is intelligent about it. He is nuanced in his complaints. He is thorough.

You're walking up San Rosendo Canyon now. The arroyo is broad, 150 yards broad in places. Rock, so much rock, and plants that have learned to love rock. Rock above and below and beside, and rock further above and below and beside all of that. Rock shorn of rock. Rock that says, "It's ok to die here." Rock that whispers, "You know it's ok to die whenever, wherever, because we'll hold you." Rock formerly known as seabed. Limestone rock. Calcium carbonate rock. Busted, held by ocotillo, dagger agave. Busted, held by desert olive, mesquite, acacia, sabal, lechugilla, candelilla. Busted, busted, beholden. The wind combing through it, past the snakes, lizards, birds, spiders, beetles, caterpillars, scorpions, tarantulas hidden in rock, the wind that rocks even your breathing to feel clumsy here.

Day six, late morning. Steady rain all night and hardest in the morning. Lee was up early this morning. He was worried, nervous that you'd be antsy and want to get some river miles in. Your canoe is better for big water than Lee's is, has more rocker, more flare up on the bow, but you recognize this, and won't urge your friend to do something that feels foolish. You're in no hurry to get off the river, no hurry at all.

You came here to listen. You wanted to hear this desert river's talk, which not just aural. The talk is visual. It's not the same talk as that on rivers back home, in the Appalachians. You hear a nourishing, soul-stirring talk when you spend time on rivers back East, but that is talk you've known for many years, it is familiar, and because of all the flora and its proximity to cities and flight paths, as well as all your memories there, it is a busier talk than that of the Chihuahua Desert.

You're here to get away from what you know. To exist in a language, so to speak, that is not your usual tongue. When Lee and you drove south and west, you could feel your alienation growing with each watershed you crossed. You looked over bridges at the rising waters, waters often running over the highway's frontage road, and there was something almost audible in your little car with the big canoes strapped to it; it was, you know, a sense of estrangement. You welcomed and you feared it.

You and Lee have paddled together often over the years. Lee is a student of rocks and understands them better than you do. He understands the processes by which they are formed and de- and re-formed. He also recognizes their component parts. He can make connections between minerals and processes. It has been a pleasure to watch him digest the place, react to its component parts. Your home watershed, the Upper James River, like this desert river, is also a limestone river, and you've been discussing the similar patterns, similar rocks, the similar but different history, that of compressed seabed, fossils, caves, carbonate.

You're here, too, because a great flood of folly and greed has swept away your family, and the only power you have in salvaging any part of it is to take care, each day, to live well and fully. That's what being a parent means now. You are still a parent, even if your kids are not speaking with you. Even if people have convinced your kids and many others in their lives that you are someone you are not, you are still a parent, and the only way to be a parent then is to be patient, which is not so different from being a parent when your kids are still in your day-to-day life.

You all check the level again. River up to the stick, same level as when you arrived at San Rosendo two days ago. This is a partial relief. You hope for more drop in the level. You hope for sun to dry the muck. Portages bear different risks here. Heroing some monster wave train with boils whirlpooling at their margins, boils long as our canoes, are risks. But ankles, busting them on mucky, slippery rocks while carrying multiple loads, that's a risk, too.

First sun now since arriving in West Texas seven days ago. Yes, the sun, now, and not one cloud. Bugs everywhere, birds giving chase. Have you only been reading this place in translation? Is this, this crazy warm brightness, the original tongue? It feels that way. Look at all the ants. Butterflies, no glance without them, and not all of them monarchs (but monarchs everywhere you look). Shadows, you almost forgot about shadows, how these crazy landforms and the plants crazy, too, cast shadows angular, singular, and also, somehow, obtuse. You can hear the place popping as it dries out. There is no original tongue. There are so many tongues.

You've laid out your wet stuff on branches. You're wearing sunglasses (somehow haven't lost them). You're going to the springs to bathe. Right there, there's a huge wasp. There's a blackbird with berry-red eyes standing on your tent's peak. You're sweating. Not thirty minutes ago you wore a winter hat. This mega-wasp wants something on your skin. Its abdomen is velvet and larger than your second-to-pinkie toe. It's not a tarantula hawk, is it?

Now the sun's almost behind the ridge. That was fast. Dagger Mountain, across the river, throws a little of its light. You're crossing the arroyo, walking from the springs back to camp. Big shadows. It almost looks misty or hazy where the sunglow crests the near ridge. The butterflies move with a quieter pace; how faultlessly they move.

Mesquite wood burning in the firepan. Last sun on Dagger Mt., still fifteen minutes of it on the north wall of San Rosendo Canyon behind us. You haven't thought of the political border in days, only of the people trying to cross it, and of the border between safe and hazardous, survival and life, timeliness and postponement, when it becomes more timely to delay, because the risk of mishap is high enough, when a mishap could mean being stuck for days, for good.

YOU WAKE TO FOG and the sound of the river, dream upwellings, feels of sorrow and longing. It's like the family court terrors of the last five years, all the false allegations and protective orders, cops and detectives and social workers at your door, at your office at work, have overnight acquired the contours of the river's flow. And the river is still so big. It rose as you slept, is back to where it was the day after its initial surge when you were up across from Maravillas. There's no way to predict what it will do.

You're eager to get back on the river. Lee is not, and so you've walked up two mesas behind camp, tracking a mule deer by its fresh droppings and prints. The fog has lifted. After a good climb, you leave the deer path to sit in a cave on a cliff, shaded, armrest of a rock and breathtaking view of San Rosendo Canyon entering the Rio. There are at least three monarch butterflies for every ten square feet of ground; how they skim in and out of the cacti and shrubs. At the cave rim, within reach, a five-forked blind prickly pear grows in a curve that suggests the prevailing winds come from downcanyon. You look out, scanning as always for movement, whether bighorn, bear, human, mountain lion, who knows. Far below, there's that ruined adobe house, the three remnant walls like a sandcastle when the incoming tide has started to wash it away.

DAY NINE, AND SUNLIGHT downclimbs Dagger Mountain's east face, the face you've been getting to know for four days. At dawn, the big moon ogled over its south flank. Now, a heavy dew. Birdsong, the river down a foot or so, more treble to its talk than the bass of yesterday. Lee's been up since dark, says, "I'm gonna lose some weight out of my boat, don't want to be pinned by an eddy. My boat's edgier than yours."

"I'm ready to get on the river whenever you say the word," you say, and then add, "I can leave in an hour or at noon or I can wait till tomorrow, but I'd rather leave today."

The sun on Dagger's face traces the profile of the mountain on which you poked around yesterday. All upstream and down, shadows of mountains on mountains. Lee's looking at the guidebook again, reads from it a sentence about whirlpools in some narrows downstream.

Soon, y'all are on the river again. It's running high but not as high as it has been. It's good paddling, and you're feeling it, loving the long wave trains of the smaller rapids, Son of Burro, Bullis Fold, Rodeo, Palmas Canyon. Lee's confidence is back. The river is good for him this way. He takes the lead, and it's fun to follow, and sometimes diverge, as he picks sneak lines around the maw of the larger rapids, all but Upper Madison Falls, which you portage.

Camp is Panther Canyon, your last night, and the stars seem to all come out at once and whisper something like, isn't this good, and hasn't it been good, and won't it be good, too, tomorrow and maybe, if you let it, every day after that.

DAWN, AND YOU HAVE a lot of miles to cover in order to meet Roy on time. You break camp with haste, tent flies still wet with dew, and start down the canyon, the river level full but good.

The morning is bend after bend, one wavetrain after another, sound of wrens and water breaking. You cover twenty miles in five hours. You run at least sixty rapids, three or four that require more than two moves. You rock your fifteen-foot canoes full of gear down S-turn after S-turn, driving into the boils below each pinch and hard stroking as if downhill on the back of the eddylines' mounded upwellings. Your mind is everywhere, nowhere. French Navy is with you, your kids are with you, all the world's lost and found. The sunlight doesn't reach the canyon's belly, through which it feels you're being ingested, until late morning.

You glance hawks, falcons, ducks, herons, lots of bugs, the green desert, strange corrugations of limestone, now beehived, chambered, other times like hornet nests. It all feels very ceramic. Swallows' nestwork. Swallows feasting on the hatching insects, landing on bent carrizo cane at the river's edge. Slap of turtles dropping into the water. The slap of the water, the silt, the good, heavy way the water with so much silt makes each stroke like planting your paddleblade in the world's guts, where whatever it means to be living on river time—love? abandon? despair? faith?—is anyone's guess.

Things to Do When You're Camped for Five Days at San Rosendo Canyon in October and Waiting for the River to Drop Out of Flood

1. Gather more firewood.
2. Lie in the hot springs with only your nose, mouth and eyes above water. Keep your ears under so you don't hear the flooded roar of the rapid. Watch out for the minnows—are they Chihuahua shiners or did you just want to say that?—that nibble your flesh, especially nipples, ears, pecker, and lips; there's one that bites more than nibbles.
3. Keep an ear tuned to San Rosendo's arroyo in case it flashes.
4. Put duct tape on stuff that could use duct tape.
5. Stare at the big muddy river and speculate on its contents and their origins.
6. Avoid the huge lumbering wasps called tarantula hawks.
7. Count butterflies, or, better yet, seek out an acacia where the monarchs are resting by the hundreds.
8. Walk down the shore and place another stick of cane at the water's edge so you can obsess further on when the river will start to drop.
9. Gather pretty stones and then, when you drop them, listen as they bounce and roll among the other pretty stones.
10. Stand in the hot springs and pump another gallon of water through your filter.

11. Think about the people back home and of how they are probably not thinking about you.
12. Walk up the mesa away from the river so you gain enough elevation to see more of the river.
13. Gather firewood.
14. Find a hook, line, and sinker while gathering firewood, and then sit in the hot springs untangling the line so you can rig it to a mesquite branch stub and then bait the hook with a chunk off your pal's sweaty summer sausage. Squat on a rock just off from the bank and hold the baited hook in an eddy. Haul in a six-pound catfish, admire and then release it back into the river alive.
15. Walk up San Rosendo Canyon yet again and wonder who left all the electrolyte water bottles and foil pounces of tuna and Doritos bags.
16. Read Yuri Herrera.
17. Speculate as to whether the river is growing more or less brown.
18. If it's cloudy and rainy, have a nap in your tent. If it's hot and sunny, nap under the cypress where springs bubble out from its roots along the river.
19. Sit with your notebook in a cave and write stuff.
20. Read yet again the guidebook about what to expect from the next 43 miles of river.
21. Guess the spot on the cliff behind which the sun will set.
22. Throw your knife at a target in the sand.
23. Hike to a cave, imagine who burned the fires there that left the coals and how long ago.
24. Wander the mesa until you find a mule deer track, fresher the better, and then follow it.
25. Pretend you are a musicologist and listen academically to the river.
26. Re-assess your food supply.
27. Take photos of flowers.
28. Drink more water, eat less.
29. Take photos of dragonflies.
30. Consider the following: if 20% of the annual rainfall has dropped since you put on the river, is the bug- and other critter-life 20% more active?

31. Poke around with your guidebook to plants of the Chihuahua desert. ID some Damiana leaves, and munch them, savor their fragrance.
32. Talk with your buddy one more time about how rare it is, and how lucky you all are, to see a green desert.

Sounds

One of the elders said: Either fly as far as you can from men, or else, laughing at the world and the men who are in it, make yourself a fool in many things.

—from *The Wisdom of the Desert Fathers, Verba Seniorum* redaction/translation by Thomas Merton

A PERSON BY A RIVER—IT MATTERS NOT WHO OR WHEN OR what river—kindled a small fire on the bank, to warm the hands. The sticks were damp. The ground was damp. Slowly, with breath, the flames enveloped the nest of smallest sticks, which were dry and dead, taken from the low flanks of a hemlock trunk. Larger sticks were laid on the nest, and their smoke was dense with the damp burning off of them. A bubbly fluid began to weep from a stick's broken edge at the side of the fire, and it dripped onto a hot ember. The ember said, Since when did a stick make rain?

Wood bears water, said the fluid.

Your water is sweet, said the ember.

I've heard tell of such sweetness, said the fluid, but it is not a thing I cultivate.

The stick cultivates it, said the ember.

What do you cultivate? asked the fluid.

Annihilation, said the ember, and ash.

That which is indestructible, said the fluid, is born in annihilation.

That sounds a little over the top, said the ember.

Most things must sound that way, from your vantage, said the fluid.

I mean, said the ember, that if you'd refrain from indulging in polysyllabic whoonaanda, I'd be more inclined to your sweetness.

Whoonaanda yourself—what's sweet to you is likely not sweet to your neighboring embers, said the fluid.

There is fire and there is heat, said the ember, but in the end there is only heat.

I don't follow you, said the fluid.

You don't know how much you follow me, said the ember.

You and I do make a fine sizzlesound, said the fluid.

There is a sizzlesound and there is vapor being made, said the ember.

But in the end, said the fluid, mockingly, there is only…

The end, said the ember. A freshness.

So, CATFISH, IS THE book not about this place? asked river.

It's about this place, yes, catfish said, and about all the places within this place.

What does that mean? asked river.

It means this place has changed over time, said catfish. A while ago, this book suggest, this place was part of a sea. There were creatures living here, and plants and stuff, that don't live here now. There were not yet the mountains, the mud and plants and other remains of that sea had not yet become rock. There were other phases after that, after the mountains formed and the sea receded, wetter phases than now, with different plants and critters.

Strange, said river, but is it a hopeful book?

I'm hopeless, catfish said, as to whether the words were given breath along the banks of the desert river—whichever bank, whichever country—or if the words gave the breath of the place some kind of echoing, at least the shadow of it.

That, river said, doesn't sound hopeless.

Maybe not, said catfish.

It was spring, rain was falling, and the institution's sprinkler system was set to run every morning from seven to eight am, no matter the weather. At roughly 8:03, a raindrop collided with the sprinkler's stream. The raindrop was surprised. It said to the sprinkler's stream, Where did you come from?

The same place as you, said the sprinkler's stream.

I highly doubt that, said the raindrop.

That highly doesn't surprise me, said the sprinkler's stream.

You come from the impoundment, right? said the raindrop.

Yes, and you are going there now, soon, said the sprinkler's stream.

I am a raindrop, said raindrop, and I was born from cloud, from weather.

I was once a raindrop, said sprinkler's stream, many raindrops, in fact.

But you've changed, said raindrop. How can you claim a past existence as having anything to do with your present state?

All present states bear history, said sprinkler's stream.

I see your point, said raindrop, and it saddens me.

Do you know your own history, asked sprinkler's stream of the raindrop.

I know that I came from the cloud. Before that, I think only the cloud knows what of me before that.

That's curious, said sprinkler's stream.

Why curious? asked raindrop.

The sprinkler system does not bear my history, said sprinkler's stream. I alone must bear it.

But wait till you evaporate and enter the cloud, said raindrop. Strange things happen in clouds.

I remember being in the cloud, said sprinkler's stream. In many clouds. They were nice places to be, and it was nice falling like you, from on high. I felt superior in ways, then, to how I feel now, all mechanized, on a timer, for dubious purposes.

What's dubious about your purpose? asked raindrop.

I've become an artificial raindrop, said the sprinkler's stream.

Like an artificial shrimp, said the raindrop.

What is an artificial shrimp? said the sprinkler's stream.

Some kind of crab or fish made to look like a shrimp, I think, said raindrop.

I remember knowing such things when I was a raindrop, said sprinkler's stream.

And do you miss such knowing, from on high, the falling-kind-of-knowing? asked raindrop.

I have forgotten how to miss things, I think, said sprinkler's stream.

Here comes the sun, said raindrop.

There it is, said sprinkler's stream.

Let it enlighten us, said raindrop.

I think it already has, said sprinkler's stream.

I feel it, said raindrop. We are enlightened, we are falling together enlightened into the soft ground. The roots will drink us both. The roots will know us as one and the same.

Or these piddly, institutional roots won't drink us, having had their fill, and we will be runoff, destined for impoundment, said sprinkler's stream.

Either way, it has been real, said raindrop.

Artificial is the new real, said spinkler's stream.

As in a dream, said raindrop.

As in an emptiness, said sprinkler's stream.

It was a warm morning for March. A tractor moved across a field, turning over the ground. Later, the field lay tilled, and rain fell for days. Even more of the pale rocks appeared on the soil than had been upturned by the tractor's implement. When the rain stopped, a large quartz crystal, with water trapped in it, lay on the sun-bathed soil.

The water trapped in the quartz was six million years old, but it hadn't forgotten how to be water. The ancient water heated in the sun, expanded, split the quartz, and spilled into the soil, which was busy losing its wetness to the sun. The soil said to the ancient water, The sun is a brute today.

If you say so, said the ancient water.

I say so, said soil. What say you?

I attend to no sun, said the ancient water.

Weird, said the soil. The sun is all we have.

The sun is not reliable, began the ancient water. What is reliable is how we attend, the choice of what to give our attention.

You are attending to me, at present, said the soil.

You bear me, at present, said the ancient water.

But the heat is bearing you, bit by bit, back into the atmosphere, said the soil.

Bit by bit, said the ancient water, so that I may attend to things above, and from above, as well as from down here.

And that is the sun's doing, said the soil just as a bird landed on the soil where the ancient water had spilled from the cracked quartz crystal. Quickly the bird took a shard of the quartz in its beak.

What are you doing, bird? asked the soil.

Gathering a bit of quartz, said the bird.

You should taste the ancient water here, said the soil.

I taste it, said the bird, in the quartz.

Is it good? asked the soil.

It is, said the bird.

Does it have my taste on it, asked the soil.

It does, said the bird, but this shard of stone has a shine that dazzles. I will use it in my nest.

Use it for what, asked the ancient water.

For delight, said the bird.

Which is the sun's doing, said the soil pointedly to the ancient water.

How, asked the ancient water, can you be so blind to the substances that formed the quartz, the substances that water bears, that you, soil, yourself, bear?

Are they not the sun's doing, asked the soil.

They are the earth's doing, said the bird.

And the earth is the sun's doing, said the soil.

No, the sun is the earth's undoing, said the ancient water.

How can you say that? asked the soil.

Sheez, said the ancient water, can't you see us losing ourselves to it?

Are you just irritated that you lost your little cocoon in the crystal?

A little bit, said the ancient water.

Did you feel more whole there? asked the soil.

I felt freed of my dreams there, said the ancient water.

So you are dreaming now

I feel awash, said the ancient water.

Awash in what? asked the bird, suddenly interested.

In all this echoing, said the ancient water.

Echoing? asked the soil.

Yes, said the last of the ancient water as it left the soil for the atmosphere.

Enough of that, said the soil.

Water goes up and water goes down, said the bird.

Is that an echo? asked the soil.

That, said the bird, is an echo.

THE FLOOD RECEDED. THE creek was a creek again. Water fanned over rocks. Many ridges and wrinkles, a soothing topography. Distraction felt viable again. No more sprawl and devour, though the ground still reeked of it. The creek said to the land, I wish the sun would dry you out.

The land said, I wish you'd stop it with all your gurgling. It's like you're some water flute. You were quieter in flood.

The creek said, You were quieter in flood, too.

The land said, That flood licked me good.

It is visible, the creek said, that licking.

The leaves have moved, said the creek. They're all matted against certain of my stones.

The land said, Those are my stones.

The creek said, Not anymore.

And my leaves, too, said the land.

Possession is boring, said the creek. Let's get on with it.

Isn't it tiresome to be always be getting on with it, said the land.

Much the opposite, said the creek.

I prefer settling in, said the land.

In some pools I settle, said the creek, and it's nice enough.

The cold will come again and settle you for a while, said the land.

Ice is bearable, said the creek.

It scours you, said the land, no?
It tenderizes, said the creek, as it does you, no?
The song the ice brings, said the land, is a pregnant one.
You mean it expands? asked the creek.
I mean it births, said the land.

COLD WINDS. ICE ON the seep's edge. First skunk cabbage with their mottled pulpits. A deer stepped in the muck and then lifted its leg out from the muck. The seep filled in the hoofprint's depression. The deer drank from it. The seep said to deertongue, I hope I taste good to you.

Always, said deertongue.

The skunk cabbage have brought their odors to the surface, said the seep.

They are gifts, said deertongue.

Their roots are quite thirsty, said the seep.

Thirst is general in such winds, said deertongue.

Do the winds drink from you, asked the seep.

Sure, said deertongue. Even the wind's roots drink from all they sink into.

How is it, really, living in a mouth? asked the seep.

Hectic! said deertongue.

How so? asked seep.

I never stop moving, said deertongue.

Have you licked a newborn fawn?

Yes.

Have you tasted blood?

Yes.

What is your favorite work?

When the deer caresses its teeth with me, I like that. I like the feel of teeth. They are my neighbors but we're so different.

I see, said the seep.

Have you tasted a newborn fawn? asked deertongue.

Duh, said the seep, I taste all things.

Not at once I hope, said deertongue.

The tastes commingle every day, in different ways, said the seep.

I like that, said deertongue.

There is much like between us, said the seep.

Nothing the matter with that, said deertongue.

After being dumped, the old broth with its rancid stench, filtered through the leaves and into the ground. Nocturnal animals were soon drawn to the place, licking and scratching at it.

An odd sort of rain must have delivered you, said ground to broth.

Broth said, And odd rains will deliver me further.

But you bear more than rain, said ground.

As do you, ground, said broth.

True, said ground, we all bear much.

Forbearance I think is the word for it, said broth.

To cease bearing, said ground, would be unbearable.

It is hard to bear either way, said broth.

To be aware of the loads I bear gives me pleasure, though, said ground.

I bear the life of a chicken, and the chicken, said broth, seems to have had a life of ranginess and nourishment, with many tasty bugs to munch.

What of the death in its life, asked ground.

Bore a fast death, painless, said broth.

I bear the sediment of a former estuary, a warm, soft place that swarmed with critters large and small, said ground.

And more recently all these leaves, said broth.

So many, and some bearing substances complex with their own bearing.

Many bearings, said broth.

Easy to forget them, said ground.

Even as we bear them, said broth.

Low Water, Loose Stone

> Solely on the Rio del Norte, which is the boundary of Nueva Vizcaya, there are so many nations that with all of their efforts the padres who were in that vicinity have not learned their names.
>
> —from a letter sent to the King of Spain
> c. 1678, quoted in *The Great River* by Paul Horgan

Your two companions, they're up as well, taking in the morning by their tents. You light your camp stove and then glance at your canoe, so yellow, almost shocking in its girth, the memory of its hull on the water, the ways it's held you, all the waves. A raven barks. The river, the desert light, everything never quite registering. You've poured water in the little pot, enough for coffee, oatmeal, too. Out here's the cream. And the sea is here, its footprint made this place. Sure, some continental plates were involved. The water bubbles, steams. Clean enough, your mug. And what of all the cane along the bank, that often are the banks? Halls of cane, aromatic as honey, corn tassel, summer. Sure, a raptor is watching you, always was. As the cane is invasive, as you are, too. Yes, the clouds are lifting. Ten more days. Have another sip, if you want.

Later, and for much of the day (and those to follow), your hands rotate along with torso and paddle, stroke after stroke. One motion, many moving parts. How many revolutions per mile the sum of the paddle's dip, purchase, uplift, reach, and then another, and so on. Little adjustments, conscious sometimes, mostly not. The neck cranes as the gaze shifts. Edges of daydream in tune, somehow, as if traversing the swirls off the stern line. You take another stroke or you don't and just drift, see bugs in sunlight, shadows reaching where they reach.

Another camp, easy enough to decide. The three of you have each other's respect and each other's backs, and it's unsaid but understood that you are here for the place as much as each other. Some nights the right bank, other nights the left—the lay of the land tells you where. You unload. You tie your boat to a paloverde, a mesquite, a boulder, something. There's stray gear in the hull, silt, a few small stones. Here's some flat ground for your tent. Soon enough, the moon's up, the bats, a little peach glow faint in the sky. Frog noise? Yes, it's January, and there's frog noise. A metal post in the boulder at river's edge, and what for makes little difference now. Sips, just sips of something good. Twilight does you like that, too, the food laid out, the pot, the spoon, the flame. Rest well, canoe, until tomorrow, carry the dew.

The river in the morning always looks a little strange, especially in mist. Looks slower. You sleep so well out here. Is it because this is home? And is that so odd, for this to be home? Someone a while back researched this river, which is a long river, and found sixteen different names in recorded history for the river, and a few come to mind now—P'Osoge, Tiguex, Río Turbio—as you go by foot up the left bank. There's ocotillo. A donkey bawls. It's hard to take a step without crushing something. These walks, often taken while waiting for the sun to crest the canyon wall. A maze of spiny things. Loose stone. A world unforgiving and fragile, crumbly, patient. Bold forms, fleshy. You cross the vega and then scramble up, stop often. The mist shifts. Green ribbon of the river, browns, tans, grays. Talus, cliff droppings. Gravel bars. Birds bray and peep. Was a kit fox down there, at the walk's outset, hardly wary of you, and why would it be—you haven't begun cheating yourself of the present moment again, have you? You reflect. The whole place, just being here, has tendered your attention. How to reflect and how to keep on. And through all this, you feel as if you could catch fire and turn to ash, as if you already have.

You squat above a spring and pump from it through a charcoal filter into a 32-ounce bottle, the fourth of twelve you'll fill and dump into a square, six-gallon container. You pump, and you think of how you've brought extra food, water, and clothing for anyone you see who might need it, though if they saw you first, as they likely would, as some might even now be staring at you, wondering, they probably wouldn't suspect you have food and water and smiles and respect for them, for their courage, their endurance, for just being alive. If they saw you now or later or saw you earlier, in your yellow canoe and your sunburnt skin and buoyant life vest, they might think you are carrying a gun, though you are not carrying a gun; and they might think you work for the government, your government (which doesn't want them to cross the river), though you don't think much of your government. If they see you, they might wonder, where is your spouse, where are your children, where is your house, your truck, your dog?

The moon rises full on this, the sixth of your ten nights. You planned this trip less around the moon than work schedules but the moon has been a vivid presence. Each evening prior to this one, the moon beamed large and radiant in the dry desert air, only setting long after you turned in. Except to read, you haven't wanted a headlamp but rather to witness this already singular, desert landscape grow even more singular with the cast of each thing—stone, cactus, shrub, cane patch—both lit and shadowed. There's a softness, an intimacy. The place feels both less and more foreign and familial. How that gossamer, silver-downiness washes out the details yet registers the essence of things, colors—violets, lavenders, grays, pales, greens—growing so tidal that each object appears accented in beforelife. Or maybe all things feel equally foreign. It feels, if you're breathing well, medicinal, like the moon's looking out for you. Your pal mentions that snakes are less active under big moons, but you know their spirits are more active, as all spirits are, even during sunlit hours those days when the moon's waxing big and you may not notice it but you know it, just feel it all day long, like some longing, love, for this, now, for life.

ANOTHER FEW HOURS ON the river, and then you leave your canoe to poke up another side canyon. Side canyons are for quiet, the river's talk out of your ear for a bit. The breezes. The bird- and bug-noise. What grows, what doesn't grow. When you try to move quickly, cover ground, all focus goes to your feet, the next step. You stop often, pause, consider the water that has moved through here, the scour patterns in the stone bed creating currents that seem to touch if not inhabit you. You stand in the aftermath of many torrents. Water moving with such force it would obliterate and sweep you into a cauldronish spume of debris. There's no water now, not even a pool, no tinaja here. You listen to rocks fall, bounce down the cliffs, and you wonder at the critter prints, scat. These are the desert's superhighways, with periodic flood maintenance. Caves are here. Up on the walls, these caves, and in them artifacts and evidence of fires can be found, lifeways imagined. You keep going. You watch your step. You can fall and break your body if you don't watch your step. You can fall and just stay here until you're outside of time, even further than you are now.

YOU SCRAMBLE TO A cave about 800 feet above camp, hoping for vistas, maybe evidence of prehistoric culture. You find vistas, yes, and artifacts, too, including a Monster energy drink can, Doritos wrappers, a hoodie, two Dulce & Gabbana faux leather coats (small and medium), some dirty socks, three voter identification cards (from the country on the other side of the river), and a length of rope. It is a sobering midden, haunting. The clothing is tucked into a cave within the cave, in a very low and deep limestone cavity, drip-textured. One of the I.D. cards is torn in half. More consonants than the names you're used to hearing. You squat there and breathe in deeply and look out over the river and cliffs. You see your pals, small figures down there at camp, the bright tents, canoes. Out loud you read the names off the cards, imagine the people who bore such names and wish them well, and then thread your way slowly back to camp.

ANOTHER MORNING, ANOTHER CANYON mouth, mile 78 or 79, the Mexico bank, and there's frost again, no mist now for days. The wind has set down. It's colder, some ice having formed overnight in the water bottles. The stars, before the moon rose, layered and dense. You stared at them for a long time. Now your pal's voice has called you to see critter tracks in the silt on the downstream end of the cobble bar, about two hundred feet from your tents. They are mountain lion tracks, unmistakable, and they're fresh, from last night or early morning. How this same pal's voice, at some point, cut through the night's pre-moon dark: "I thought I'd seen stars, but now I've seen stars."

LATER, THE BIGHORN, FOUR of them. They stare at you. You stare at them. You're in the runout of yet another long wave train. The present has sucked you in. The present, in a desert canyon many miles from—or closer to?—nowhere, no roads, no phone service. Sucked in, or is it something else? Have things fallen apart? Could things fall apart out here? Could you be nailed to the present? You go on, another stroke, and another, and listen as the river—this wound, this balm—tells you its names, and then erases them.

And Echoes

> For those whose goal is an end to conflict, then, better to become intimate with the self that clings to difference. And better to forget about it.
>
> —Lewis Hyde

So you're telling me, catfish, that the book contains lots of conversations between water and things that exist in and by water.

Yes, said catfish. Like between me and you, now, yes.

Conversations that take place here? asked river.

Here and not here, said catfish, with the not here being what is here but is no longer except in memory. And about what is here but originated from upstream of here.

Whose memory? asked river.

The rocks mostly, said catfish.

Like in the fossils and stuff? asked river.

Yes, from when there was a sea here, like I said earlier, and from after that, said catfish, when it rained here more often and there were more and very different plants.

As in landscapes that still exist, asked river, but no longer exist here?

Yes, said catfish.

That is curious, said river.

Seems it is, said catfish, a curious kind of listening.

But all listening is curious, no? asked river.

Unfortunately not, said catfish.

You mean like if something is listening, river said, but only to hear more clearly what it's already thinking?

Something like that, said catfish.

THE STONE, AND THE rubber drawn taut. The lake, the light, the small human. One elbow locked, the other cocked tight. And then the tremor, the wished-for destination. The pouch released. Slap of rubber. The stone gone, lost to sight. And finally the small splash.

Bring any doughnuts? lake asks stone.

Not a one, says stone.

Shoot, says lake.

That's over, says stone.

Shot, says lake, you done been.

How long is this falling going to take? asks stone.

How long you want it to take? asks lake.

Well, says stone, I'm not a fan of bottoms.

My bottom is right squishy, says lake.

Most are, says stone.

You know a lot of bottoms? asks lake.

Too many, says stone.

Strange, says lake.

What's strange? asks stone.

That you've been travelling from bottom to bottom, says lake, is strange.

Not unusual, says stone, being a fragment of a once-bottom. More pressure at the bottom, says lake.

Never minded my origins, being snuggled, says stone.

How about bringing doughnuts next time, says lake.

Do my best, says stone.

Darker down here, says lake.

Dark is light to me, says stone.

How so? asks lake.

My kind the dark makes, says stone.

A lot of kinds of dark, says lake.
Dark and depth be buds, compress stuff, says stone.
And over time, much time, says lake, stuff hardens.
Sure enough, says stone.
Enough of the old ways, says lake.
Dream on, buddy, says stone.
I will, says lake, like for a slingshot that launches doughnuts.
Well, doughnuts, says stone, they likely float.

AND, MEANWHILE, THE PLASTIC quart bottle of oil was not fully drained, nor was its lid affixed, when it was tossed in the river just upstream of aforementioned little dramas. As the river entered the quart bottle, the oil said, We are like from such totally different planets.

Not so, said the river.

How not, asked the oil.

Said the river, Much of my water was used to enable your extraction.

Said oil, Am I supposed to give you a medal?

I can't wear medals, said the river.

Aren't you polluted already, like the moment you emerge from the ground? asked the oil.

These days it could be argued so, said the river.

No so in other days? asked the oil.

Not so much, said the river.

But no poets sung of you then, said the oil.

Plenty did, said the river, in many languages.

More languages than now? asked the oil.

Many more languages, said the river. And it was easier to hear them.

Did you sing along with them? asked the oil.

I am still singing along, said the river, to those old songs in the lost languages—it is my truest calling.

Why not mix it up with the present songs? asked the oil.

The lost languages won't allow it, said the river.

Or you won't allow it? asked the oil.

They don't mix, said the river.

But not mixing is a form of mixing, no? said the oil.

Mixing is mixing, said the river, and not mixing is not mixing.

You sound foolish, said the oil.

Of course I do, said the river.

Why of course? asked the oil.

Because you can't hear me, said the river.

But we are having a conversation, said the oil.

We are, yes, but we cannot mix, said the river.

So what we discuss has no meaning? asked the oil.

Exactly, said the river.

You are impossible, said the oil.

We are impossible, said the river.

But your water enabled my existence, said the oil.

Please, said the river, forget I mentioned it.

I won't forget, said the oil, and I won't forget how offended I am feeling.

You are the offense, said the river.

No, my extraction was the offense, said the oil, and you were a tool in that.

See, said the river, we cannot mix.

It was winter, breezy. A small mammal traversed the slope from a place at the cliff base. It stretched its neck and with its tongue began to lap from a seep's deeper recess.

Don't overdo it, said seep.

What's done is over, said small mammal.

Doing, though, said seep, is best under.

The sun, when it is under, still drinks, small mammal said.

Have you asked the trees? seep said.

They announce it nightly, said small mammal.

But not as much, said seep, as in the daytime.

Your water is bright, said small mammal.

It shines in part, said seep, from your light.

But there is heaviness, too, said small mammal, in every sip.

And you lift it and then you send it down, seep said.

So it happens, said small mammal.

As it always will, said seep.

I sense many others, said small mammal.
Many tongues know my voice, said seep.
And your brightness, said tongue.
Which is only waves, said seep.
And nourishment, said small mammal.
Sure, said seep.

FROM UPSTREAM DRIFTS NOW some old dead branch, pale and smooth. It tremors and turns in the outflow of a frothy chute. The river is wide here, and swift and rocky.
What news do you bring, river asks.
Becoming news, says driftwood.
Please, river says, elaborate.
News of diminishment, says driftwood, and of becoming.
So you prefer that I leave you be? asks river.
More that you see me as yourself, says driftwood, and as equally alien and fresh.
But you are born from roots, says river.
As are you, driftwood says.
A branching of tributaries, says river.
Branching like all roots do, and going far beneath, says driftwood.
Such is becoming, says river.
And diminishing, says driftwood.
I like the late light up there on that long, headwalled ridge, says river.
Or do you like how becoming liking it is, asks driftwood.
Toward liking it I feel nothing, only toward the light do I feel a pull, says river.
So many pulls, says driftwood.
Is it the pull or the pulling, asks river.
Is what the pull or the pulling, asks driftwood.
Is the meaning in the pull or the pulling, asks the river.
There is care in the pulling, and in the pulls there's more attraction than care, says driftwood.
Easier, then, to let go of the pulling, wonders river.
What pulls is, perhaps, what we've been taught can pull, says driftwood.

I'm not so sure about that, says river.
Even your doubt is pulling, says driftwood.

FURTHER NORTH, AMONG LONG ridges and small creeks, the goose noticed a pond. But for the brief, straight line of a dam above a narrow and rocky gorge, the pond's shape resembled a kidney. Still, the shape was pleasing enough, and the goose landed in it.

What's the news from above, the pond asked.

Nothing going on that you don't already reflect, said the goose.

So you feel at home, said the pond.

I feel more like a duck than a goose, said the goose, but that's been the deal for a while.

So it's a homey feeling, began the pond, to the feel more like a duck than a goose, even though you look and talk, fly, land and feed like a goose?

It's a feeling, said the goose, that's hard to describe.

Like being lost, maybe, said the pond.

Being lost, said the goose, is simply being honest about being.

I don't feel lost, said the pond.

But you might could *be* lost, said the goose.

I'm no longer creek and not quite lake, said the pond.

You are impounded, said the goose, and then dipped its head beneath for a meal.

You are confounded, said the pond.

Maybe, but I find your shallows very nourishing, said the goose.

Imagine my depths, said the pond.

If only I could dive that far down, said the goose.

You'd need to feel more like an otter than a goose who feels like a duck. Or perhaps grebe fantasies would suffice, said the pond.

I sense your hate, said the goose.

You could call it fear as well, said the pond.

Impoundment, said the goose, is what I'll call it.

CRAWDAD MOSEYED UP FROM its den beneath the bottom of the river and noticed smallmouth noodling a hellgrammite from under a nearby boulder.

Haven't seen you since the flood, said crawdad.

Crazy how many shades we inhabit, said smallmouth.

I don't catch your drift, said crawdad.

And how many gradations of sand, said smallmouth.

Even so, crawdad began, the swarm factor sure has mellowed since I last saw you.

Lost voices of the original stones, said smallmouth.

Easier to meal now, said crawdad.

I'm not talking about the place where rocks are born, said smallmouth.

You don't seem to be talking with me at all, said crawdad.

There's a fresh hellgrammite in my belly, smallmouth said.

And that affects how you converse with your neighbor? asked crawdad.

A river is many villages, said smallmouth.

Like Swimming Underwater Except it Gives You Breath

> "Locally extinct?" "No," he said. He waved his extended left hand quickly in a sweeping arc. "It's all out there, everywhere."
>
> —Barry Lopez

LAST OF THE DAY'S SUN BRUSHES THE SIERRA DEL CARMEN, that long wall snowy and surf-like on the horizon. Nearer faces, those of the canyon and the canyon's sidecanyons, grow steeped in shade, and with the twilight glow their textures appear more distinct and more endless, too.

Now a phoebe at river's edge, late December sky losing its blue, though maybe the floodplain, where the borders of things are fading into lavender, is in some hurry not to. You sit in it, on a cobble bank's flank. How smooth the stones, how many expressions they make, hues. Raven gutterals begin from back of camp, some cliff. Sounds as if the bird's asking where what says begins, whether the echos, the untalk, or what.

Started down the river about five hours ago, after being dropped at the access in Big Bend National Park by Roy Englesdorf who with his wife Ruth runs the Outback Oasis Motel and Snake Room in Sanderson, Texas. This is first camp (big cobblebar, mouth of a sidecanyon), and it's good, so good to be back in Boquillas Canyon. The place has stayed close, and in surprising ways over the four years since you first canoe tripped through it, has drawn you back twice for twenty days in the Lower Canyons, downstream of here, and has also helped ground and buoy you through the day-to-day back home.

After being apart for half a decade (during which time you faced your ex in over twenty-five court dates) your two youngest kids, 10-year-old boy and girl, twins, live with you every other week now, have for over a year, a miracle of sorts, a strenuous one.

You all have spent many days of the last year or so exploring local rivers in small boats, and in winter you all explore the banks and tributaries, hunting rocks, driftwood, other wonders. You've thought some today about your readiness for exploring this place together (they are with their mom and you, each, for two weeks, now, at the winter holiday). There's not one deciding factor, rather a swarm of details, hunches, feels. Can we carry enough water in our boats? Is the weather, not just meteorological, too shifty? If one of us is injured, what will we do? Who might come with us whom we'd all enjoy, trust?

Such thoughts, if not all thoughts, flow through the background in a place like this, as the landscape is demanding physically and aesthetically, in a frank, clarifying way. There's something of the nude about a desert canyon, something both shocking and intimate, detached and seductive, especially if you live far away in mountains with similar geological DNA but of a very different age and with dense soil and flora covering them.

First morning to wake on the river. A deep, restful sleep. The breeze has grown more spirited, and blows from the west, upstream; mesquite branches wear it in their sway. The canoe's still here, tied fast to a boulder. The silt (there's no sand here) remains damp from the snow and rain of three days prior. Dregs of last night's fire in the pan, smoked herring cans burnt and curled among the ashes. Tent fly flutter, that nylon crinklesound. Sun is up, not yet down here in the canyon, and already a new country reveals its layers, an old country, too.

Up the sidecanyon, now, for a jaunt, each step's grinding thwips and thwacks on the graylavendar gravel of its wash. Inside the first bend off the river, where the sidecanyon oxbows back west, you sit, watching the sun skin the peach of the river canyon's far wall. Time's funnelings, and weather's, the breeze still from upstream. This wall—or call it a face, a mural of faces—the one you lean against, shadow-outlined on that one.

Feels like you're always in a wave down here, a wave curling so patiently it would take far more than your children's children to know its final foam. You poke among the stone forms, the hoodoos and keyholes, all the slots and grottoes off of and in the sidecanyon, as if some googly-eyed reef dweller. This dun shine, all this hardness and fracture and glow. And no soil below, no roots, unless petrified.

The barrel cactus' hot pink spines, the lechugilla's modes of spike. You swell here and tread, puffered and goof. You come a long way from home, sometimes, only to feel more at home. Time's the subject. The way other lives, future and former, feel embedded here, seeded, embodied, too. You'd love to see your kids open up to this, for this to be available to them, to be felt, however they may feel it, and for them to know themselves here, in this landscape and then back home, in their two homes, with this landscape and its lives and deaths in them.

The cliff fragments' strike-slip filigree. Shards of fossil—clam, oyster, ammonite, etc.—under most every step. And, meanwhile, the river's dimplings, all the acoustics, metaphysics of echo. How seeing in this place expands via compression of vista by canyonwalls, jaw sore from staring, craning. If the body feels geological here, it's not (or maybe it is, you're no expert), but the ribcage, the pelvic floor, marrow's sediment—you just have to walk with it. No matter what movement or stillness, it's hard to escape the urgency and patience, the stories and futures, in all this rock.

Good miles today, canyon-by-canoe miles, easy paddling. Look ahead a little, look back up, down, around. Faces from and at all angles and lights, shadow. Not much to say, the wind says it pretty much nonstop.

Ten miles or so travelled before second camp, a grassy bench a hundred feet from the bank. A nest of a spot for the tent, willow-walled. Next terrace up, a sidecanyon's blowout sprawls, pale guts of bedrock busted, some storm god's flood dust.

Spires on the opposite canyon wall, spires a hundred feet tall, with narrower spires reaching off of those spires. So many wonders in the weatherings of carboniferous, in what wears off and what remains. Your kids, total rockhounds, would love to see this. They have weathered much and will weather more, as all beings do. The times are gusty and apt to sudden floods, if not drought. And look at the lower slopes, between the cliff faces and river plain, how gravelly they are, lechugilla-pocked.

What the battered, old boot upstream at the abandoned candelilla wax camp said, "Desert rivers hardly know crap, and you even less." What the gar skull in the trash midden said, "Time to fix time once and for all."

If the art of good camp is symmetry, and if symmetry in camp is as much setup as chance and patience, then so be it. There were three other places upstream, each good for camp, but this one, of course, is very fine. Anyway, there's no bad camp, no camp that happens in bad.

Hot little blaze in the firepan and a steady, mild breeze from the south; some might call it wind. Though mild, the air cuts cool enough to spark a windchill. Cuban coconut beans rehydrated for dinner, a beer. Stars like a bag of spilled sugar, a bag big as vision itself. Is it Milky Way or further stars, those densities of twinkle? Or is it what juices the stone's thick, what juices the brokenness? No saner densities.

Saw a foal nursing off its white mare yesterday, up the sidecanyon before we broke camp. They stood on the busted stone, lower legs lost in pricky pear and ocotillo, the mom leaning her head on her offspring's back as it supped. The kids would have loved seeing that. Even now, you're seeing them seeing that in some constellation.

SLOW MORNING, COFFEE AND grub and walks, before it's time to break it all down. You start with the tent, upstake and depole it, and then leave it lying and walk down the cobblebar where the bluff at the edge of it drops down to the river with its aquamarine and sluggish, low flow. The forms currents have made there, in the silt, the chunks of bark-stripped tree, also limbs with their greenery—salt cedar?—sorted and piled on the silt according to direction and size. Seems to be evidence that last night, while all around was being punctured a trillion times by the stars, a beaver, maybe more than one, was down here munching, all lit up.

You head back, roll up the tent with its poles and stakes, and slide it in its nylon package, fat cigar. Next, the food box, the water jugs, the glances at the canyonwall, the sky, or upstream to the corrugations of shine on the river's rippled bend. Or just down at the shadows of the willow branches bending in the wind on the sleeping pad being rolled now, deflated and rolled some more.

Before long, the canoe's loaded and launched. The first paddle strokes to stretch you out, every departure a confluence of reflection and anticipation. Soon, the miles drift on, simple and packed.

WHY CANOE, WHY HERE in a desert to travel by canoe? Why canoe at all? To see what water has made of the land, and to feel those remnant waters? To be uncreated? To know the river as the former life, how the river does not lead to but is the former life and this one and the deaths in them and in the future ones? And for the moments unbubbling into moments bubbling again?

You canoe because most days it feels like there's so much love in your torso it could jumpstart an aircraft carrier. You canoe for the seeing in glances and in the staring. You canoe to find a way out from inside the noise. Is it rock you canoe, or is it river, is it surf or is it paddle, revel, is it trees or critters or shiver; it is plant and stone, bones and sliver?

You canoe for the passion of being freed from passion. To do no evil, to purify time, to undo craving. To digest the reading, to feel the designer's desire in every part of the craft, the paddle, and the place. To read the digesting by the place of its past every moment being made. For the cherry light on the stones, the pockets of shadow, the wet spots, the dry, the turds, the births, the flesh and throat's response to the air bearing it all, all it may.

And for the surprises you canoe. For the river to river you wave, chute, eddy, pool, and bed. You canoe to carry plenty of water over the damaged water, to stay hydrated here in this land of little rain, and for the sleep after the miles, the headwind, the cadence of the lift and purchase of the blade. And for the emptying and the loading again of the canoe. You canoe to awaken a tenderness.

You canoe for the newly fallen across and in the river and the decision of when and how to skirt and bless such gifts, such obstructions. And to share the pleasure of the canoe's motion on the water with everyone who knows that such pleasure is not all sensual. You canoe to be in touch with the majestic drift and the majestic uselessness.

For to know the sides of the river, some cinnamon worship, a centering. For the full continuous thank you of the being alive in it. And sometimes from the canoe you snap bad pics of the corridor as it swallows you like a snack. You are in awe before the awe of it all, and canoe to know the changing moistures, the nature of root and stone, and often are in stitches before the loaded hull's scratches and dents.

For the filaments of passing glances, how they combine and drift, disperse and congeal. All the ecologic intimacies and stuff, the integrated watershed dynamics, not apart but with. You canoe to be inside as much as out, and to go with that being into its outsides and ins, being's. You canoe for the distances and distance's closenesses. You canoe to hock up the gunk. You canoe for the hug, for the wind's hug is forgiveness, as the water's is, too.

For the brethrening and the curves and the straights and the drops. To return, to feel the saner velocities, without hope. To bed in the body of motion and to rest after such motion in the momentum of stillness. To remember the bone's componentry. To praise the paddle's simplicity as you stroke and drift. You praise the straps with which the gearbags are lashed to the thwarts. And, stroking again, to etch the breath with the edge's tablature.

O, canoe, big and leaky, to ride the river in you, to be erased, to read, be read and rewritten. And to know the canoe canoeing back to be carved in and out of the always eddying gradient, reshaped, as the undrifted dispersal of all tumblehome meeting the resistances. You canoe for the drift's hope, but it is the hull's integrity, not hope, that floats us at all.

And for the sound, though canoes don't make sound. The sound of a canoe is the sound of water. The sound of a canoe is the sound of its machine. The sound of a canoe's machine is the sound of a person driving the canoe. The sound of a person driving a canoe is the sound of that person stirring the river with a paddle. The sound of a paddle stirring the river is the sound of a stirred thing being stirred. The sound of a stirred thing being stirred is the sound of much stirring, and stirs much.

Like the passing bees nest. The turkeys, the javelinas, the zone-tailed hawk. Running up onto the gravelbar before the strainer-choked bend. For eddying out because big bear's on one side of the river and cubs on the other. For the highwater lines, the cutbanks, the water's load, sediment and molecule. To know the changes in every crease and upwelling. To heat the grease the kneecaps are packed in. To become unheeled. To thank the gunwale. To become let in.

And to kneel, and reach, kneeling, hip-swiveling amongst the knock-kneed rocks. The way waves slap the hull. The longest shortcomings. Canoe the vehicle that seduces its fuel, drifts on its engine. Canoe patient in the transference of there into here & here & here. Canoe, here, you are holy ovalness of angles, vectoring. Here, canoe, you are becoming so many onenesses vaguely tasting of salt—or is it steel?—riverborne neither north nor south nor toward nor from but all of the below.

Good miles, strange trances, daydreams, riffles, brainwaves, stroke after stroke, and now it's time to break. You drive the bow onto another cobblebar. Typical stuff: stones, silt, horse crap, some drift. You note the mesquite, acacia, carizzo cane (border bamboo), various small bones. The cobblebar part of a big island, twenty feet above waterline at peak, driftwood mats tangling shrubs at the upstream edge of the peak. It's lunchtime. You eat, stare, and it's good.

Two falcons ride the south breeze along the canyonwalls' fissured contours. A bit of a nap and then a wander down the island, stopping to stare down, reach, examine various stones. Walking feels good, a little funny. Eyes on some wonder, you nearly stumble on a carcass. The long legs and tail, the small skull, that one ear, the leather of it—gracious, there's no question. But it wasn't full grown, the mountain lion, maybe forty pounds before it came to permanent, silted rest on a cobblebar, fur still on paws, legs, back, tail. Its repose a posture of leap, no sign of wound, though one canine appears mighty worn, too small perhaps to function. It's been a dry year here, too, five inches of rain total in the last 368 days, so maybe there just wasn't enough food.

Or maybe it broke its neck or jaw and starved. The mountain lion, which like this river has many names—panther, painter, cougar (Amazonian roots), puma (Incan roots), Mexican lion, swamp screamer, deer lion—hunt by stealth, timing, and impact. Their lung-capacity unfit for chase, they creep close, then burst, with their strong collarbones, upon the necks of deer and javelina, their usual prey here, and sometimes the bounty is large, or the strike is off a hair, and the cougar's jaw breaks, or the neck.

Droughts are ghosts, as floods are, and everything else out here, and ghosts live and die every breath. You don't want to leave this place either, little lion, and don't think you have; you're here, your trot and stare, your stalk and crouch and leap, in all that's cracked and solemn, grave and spare, cementing and breaking, conjugating itself ad infinitum and whole.

In the greens that light up this place after rare rains, in every gesture of this vast patience and quiet.

In the crags.

In all that remains, elegies to what has been and is still being scooped and deposited, birthed and swept away.

You MOVE ON DOWNSTREAM in the canoe, feeling grave, honored, foolish, alive. Little by little, as the canyonwalls descend, the horizon stretches out. Everything seems overexposed, as if not just the vista has lost its frame, its filter. There's no going back, only coming back, and that'll be a while.

Now out of the canyon, you notice, for the first time this trip, empty water bottles and electrolyte wrappers. You think of the kids, curious how they'd experience this place between countries, where borderness is both more real and more abstract than on a road, in a city or airport, amongst signs, a wall, passport checks. They'd see here that, physically, whether you camp on river left or river right, a border is arbitrary, and that rivers make convenient borders. They'd see birds and wind and these feral and winter grazing horses and burros and cattle crossing back and forth through the shallow river. And see the signs of people crossing, having crossed.

When they first explored the Chattooga River, river of your heart, border between South Carolina and Georgia, the kids were often very curious what side they were on, what state, but soon that aspect of it moved to the background. It's good, in part, to have a sense of border that's rooted in watershed consciousness, divides between waterways, as well as politics. Of course, your kids would notice the water bottles and electrolyte wrappers left on the bank, and you'd talk about it.

They know on a deep level, your kids, the borders defined by marriage, and they're aware that their dad crossed that border when they were young, and how this choice has caused you all (and the extended families) suffering. What they are learning now, too, perhaps, is how a border, whether honored or crossed or both, is always a source of suffering and possibility, perhaps even safety.

They'd be curious about why people are coming to America, risking their lives to walk through this unforgiving place without a canoe to hold ample water, gear, food, etc. Walking across hundreds of miles of desert on either side, many assaulted, injured, or dying along the way, some making it across only to be detained, questioned, and sent back to the same, if not worse hell.

You'd offer thoughts in small doses. Many people's lives are intolerable, you'd tell them. They cannot make a living in their home countries, cannot feed their children, nor often themselves. Many, in fact, are children, many under threat from gangs. They have been threatened with death. They have been assaulted and beaten. Their family members have been killed. Their lives are incomprehensible. They seek refuge.

Of course, your kids would notice the agents with their dogs, armor, and machine guns at the border patrol station one drives through on the way back to Roy and Ruth's motel after obtaining the river permit at the Big Bend Visitor Center, and they might ask, "Is this what the U.S. is doing about the border?"

In part, you'd say, yes, and then refer them to the books on our shelves at home, books that share each in their heart- and mind-wrenching, intelligent ways the impossibly complex, tender, and brutal stories of the border, books by Fernando Flores, Valeria Luiselli, Anthony Cody, Javier Zamora, Luis Alberto Urrea, Charles Bowden, Yuri Herrera, Eduardo Corral, Gloria Anzaldua, Sebastian Rotella, and others.

And you'd list some of the documentary movies that are available for us to watch, like *No Le Digas A Nadie/Don't Tell Anyone*, *Inocente*, *Who is Dayani Cristal*, *The Other Side of Immigration*, *Which Way Home*, and others. And tell them about the people working along the border to serve those who cross, organizations (like Val Verde Border Humanitarian Coalition in Del Rio) with volunteers and activists who offer aid, from legal to medical to clothing, food, water, shelter, and many other forms of help. And you'd remind them how you've brought extra water food and clothes for anyone you all might meet.

CAMP AGAIN ON THE river right bank, a small butte visible just above the flat where you set the tent, views from it all around, to distant and solitary peaks, to the Sierra del Carmen, its limestone bands, sculpted flanks, the mesa stretching out into the haze. Dun expanses. Golden cane that marks the corridor. Different raven probably, but the same old squawk.

A world of rock. Not much moves but the river and the breeze and the things they move. But you feel the movement because you see the patterns of it in everything. Time's erosion maps each place the eyes fall. The eyes, they fall, they fall and fly. They drift. You'd have to sit a long time to see the rainbow cactus send out the growth of one entire spine, but it's a pretty evening, your last out here for a while, so why not try.

Twice

A TEAR FELL INTO THE BRACKISH WATER OF THE MARSH JUST as the tide was starting to turn. Soon, an oyster sucked the tear into its yumspace. The tear felt many things inside the oyster. Oyster, noticing the tear, said, How's your day going?

Mighty fine, said tear. And yours?

Same old, said oyster. I'm glad the tide is turning.

I bet you are, said tear.

What do you know of tides? asked oyster.

I am a product of tides.

You mean the moon drives you, too?

Of course, said tear.

I wasn't aware of that, moon said.

Tear said, I wasn't either, but being in your yumspace has showed me.

That's good to hear, said oyster.

It's good to feel, said tear, to feel that I've grown closer to my origins.

Your origins are far away, no? said oyster.

Grief birthed me, said tear, but the moon birthed the grief.

Perhaps the sun birthed the moon, said oyster.

Perhaps the marsh birthed the body that channeled the grief birthed by the moon, tear said.

Perhaps the body that channeled the grief is closer now than before, even if the body has moved far inland, oyster said.

Maybe so, said tear.

This is going to be a good flood tide, oyster said. There is much aswirl.

I have been birthed by other bodies channeling grief and by some bodies channeling joy and some even that were channeling desperation, said tear, so I know swirl.

This body of mine, said oyster, is too close to swirl to really know it.

But soon you will spit me out, no, asked tear.

Naturally, I will spit out part of you, said oyster, and part of you will remain with me.

I will be two places at once then, said tear.

You will be one in two places, said oyster.

As in twice whole, asked tear, such as both wings of your shell?

It is happening now, started oyster. Do you feel yourself becoming half the tear you used to be?

I feel the same, said tear, but I feel it twice.

Acknowledgments

Thanks to my companions on the river and on the long drives to and back from it; to my colleagues at Hollins University, with special thanks to the Swannanoa gang and to the administration and board of trustees for sabbatical time and assistance with travel and research; to my best reader and bow partner (on all rivers figurative and literal), Jessie van Eerden; to my friends and colleagues, Jon Guy Owens and Morgan Wilson for crucial gear loans and support; to my family for everything and everything else, always; to Adam Moseley for wise counsel; to Crispin Harwell for keeping the wheels and smiles rolling; to Marc W. McCord, Louis F. Aulbach, Joe Butler, Roland Wauer, and Carl M. Fleming for your invaluable trip reports and guides to the river and the life along and in it; to the good people staffing Big Bend National Park, as well as the motels, gas stations, and other services along the way from Roanoke, VA, west to Sanderson, TX, especially during COVID; to Dede Cummings for great cover design; to my students and to the authors and translators whose work involving the border we read and discussed – Gloria Anzaldúa, Eduardo Corral, Lisa Dillman, Dolores Dorantes, Fernando Flores, Yuri Herrera, Valeria Luiselli, Manuel Portillo, John Pluecker, Sara Uribe, among others; and to the editors of the journals where some of these works first appeared: Patagonia's *The Cleanest Line*, *Pine Row Press*, *Scoundrel Time*, *storySouth*, and *The Concho Review*.

www.ingramcontent.com/pod-product-compliance
Lightning Source LLC
Chambersburg PA
CBHW020917090426
42736CB00008B/669